Dynamics of Discernment

POSTMODERN ETHICS SERIES

Postmodernism and deconstruction are usually associated with a destruction of ethical values. The volumes in the Postmodern Ethics series demonstrate that such views are mistaken because they ignore the religious element that is at the heart of existential-postmodern philosophy. This series aims to provide a space for thinking about questions of ethics in our times. When many voices are speaking together from unlimited perspectives within the postmodern labyrinth, what sort of ethics can there be for those who believe there is a way through the dark night of technology and nihilism beyond exclusively humanistic offerings? The series invites any careful exploration of the postmodern and the ethical.

Series Editors:
Marko Zlomislic (Conestoga College)
† David Goicoechea (Brock University)

Other Volumes in the Series:

Cross and Khôra: Deconstruction and Christianity in the Work of John D. Caputo edited by Neal DeRoo and Marko Zlomislić

Agape and Personhood with Kierkegaard, Mother, and Paul (A Logic of Reconciliation from the Shamans to Today) by David Goicoechea

The Poverty of Radical Orthodoxy edited by Lisa Isherwood and Marko Zlomislić

Theologies of Liberation in Palestine-Israel: Indigenous, Contextual, and Postcolonial Perspectives edited by Nur Masalha and Lisa Isherwood

Agape and the Four Loves with Nietzsche, Father, and Q (A Physiology of Reconciliation from the Greeks to Today) by David Goicoechea

Fundamentalism and Gender: Scripture—Body—Community edited by Ulrike Auga, Christina von Braun, Claudia Bruns, and Jana Husmann

Dynamics of Discernment

A Guide to Good Decision-Making

STEPHEN J. COSTELLO

Foreword by John Hill

☙PICKWICK *Publications* • Eugene, Oregon

DYNAMICS OF DISCERNMENT
A Guide to Good Decision-Making

Postmodern Ethics Series 13

Copyright © 2022 Stephen J. Costello. All rights reserved. Except for brief quotations in critical publications or reviews, no part of this book may be reproduced in any manner without prior written permission from the publisher. Write: Permissions, Wipf and Stock Publishers, 199 W. 8th Ave., Suite 3, Eugene, OR 97401.

Pickwick Publications
An Imprint of Wipf and Stock Publishers
199 W. 8th Ave., Suite 3
Eugene, OR 97401

www.wipfandstock.com

PAPERBACK ISBN: 978-1-6667-3016-6
HARDCOVER ISBN: 978-1-6667-2130-0
EBOOK ISBN: 978-1-6667-2131-7

Cataloguing-in-Publication data:

Names: Costello, Stephen J., author.

Title: Dynamics of discernment : a guide to good decision-making / by Stephen J. Costello.

Description: Eugene, OR: Pickwick Publications, 2022 | Postmodern Ethics Series 13 | Includes bibliographical references and index.

Identifiers: ISBN 978-1-6667-3016-6 (paperback) | ISBN 978-1-6667-2130-0 (hardcover) | ISBN 978-1-6667-2131-7 (ebook)

Subjects: LCSH: Enneagram | Decision making | Discernment | Creative ability

Classification: HD30.23 C67 2022 (print) | HD30.23 (ebook)

09/15/22

Dr Costello's book alerts us to a subject that concerns the very core of our existence. This book is well-written, has clear focus, and makes effective use of other philosophical and religious sources, both East and West. One might be overwhelmed by all the lists that are part of the decision-making process, but it is precisely through pondering on these lists, the reader can gain insight into the complexities of decision-making. With the precision of a surgeon's knife the author describes the dynamics of this process as an inter-play between the discriminating powers of the conscious mind and the stillness of a deeper self that can be awakened through meditation and other forms of mental practices. Doctor Costello reminds us that when making an important decision we need to live in the here and now, and not in a past or future.

Besides a rich philosophical amplification, the reader will find in Dr Costello's book solid, practical advice when it comes to actual decision-making: Consider what good does it bring to you and the other; don't decide when you are 'lost, lethargic or low'; don't rely on momentary feelings, which is to be distinguished from Carpe Diem (the imperative of the instant); above all be honest and authentic. Dr Costello brings to our attention the ethical component in decision making. He addresses the need to address the plight of 'the minority group, the ostracized, the stranger the widow, the orphan'. Dr Costello reminds us to keep in mind, what Jungians call the shadow: Our biases, hidden motivations, and ignorance. When focussing on the final end of life, a spiritual quality of decision-making shines forth: What will be my legacy to the world?

The many lists that the reader encounters in this book are not to be interpreted in terms of factual knowledge, rather as elements that activate or inspire a decision-making process. This process is not simply assessing the externalities of the situation, but, following Jung's notion of the transcendent function, we need to be aware of an inner dialogue between consciousness and the creative unconscious to face the unexpected. Early humankind were aware of this kind of dialogue and invested a lot of energy in creating divination techniques to make the decision-making process more conscious. One the most sophisticated of early divination techniques was the *I Ching*. Dr Costello has written an interesting chapter on the *I Ching* and the *Tarot* and their relevance today, as found in the works of Jung, Progoff and Valentin Tomberg.

The author ends with a brilliant description of the triune brain, capturing the complexity of the decision-making process in terms of brain-functioning. Even if 'the undisputed champion of the triune brain is the reptilian brain', Dr. Costello advocates an alignment of all three parts of the brain in the decision-making process. As we execute our choices, we are engaging in a process of creating ourselves to be who we are. I recommend this book to all who wish to know more about the choices they have made and will continue to make as they discover who they are and who they want to become.

—John Hill

I dedicate this book to my parents, Val and Johnny,
in loving gratitude and enduring admiration.

Good decisions come from experience. Experience comes from making bad decisions.

—Mark Twain

Our bodies are our gardens to which our wills are gardeners.

—William Shakespeare

When making a decision of minor importance, I have always found it advantageous to consider all the pros and cons. In vital matters, however, such as the choice of a mate or a profession, the decision should come from the unconscious, from somewhere within ourselves. In the important decisions of personal life, we should be governed, I think, by the deep inner needs of our nature.

—Sigmund Freud

The impediment to action advances action. What stands in the way becomes the way.

—Marcus Aurelius

Contents

Acknowledgments | ix
Foreword by John Hill | xi
Introduction | xiii

1 On Choosing and Deciding | 1
2 Enneagram Discerning | 50
3 Creativity | 63
4 Applying Theory U | 87
5 Synchronicity | 95
6 The Triune Brain | 112

Bibliography | 123

Acknowledgments

I WOULD LIKE TO express my sincere gratitude to my parents first and foremost—Val and Johnny—for their encouragement and sustained interest in my work, and to whom I dedicate this book. Thank you to my friends too, especially Darren Cleary and Derek Smyth, for their ongoing support over many years. I am indebted, too, to Michael Ryan's philosophical counsel and remain deeply appreciative to you all.

Foreword

DR. COSTELLO'S BOOK ALERTS us to a subject that concerns the very core of our existence. This book is well-written, has clear focus, and makes effective use of other philosophical and religious sources, both East and West. One might be overwhelmed by all the lists that are part of the decision-making process, but it is precisely through pondering on these lists, the reader can gain insight into the complexities of decision-making. With the precision of a surgeon's knife the author describes the dynamics of this process as an inter-play between the discriminating powers of the conscious mind and the stillness of a deeper self that can be awakened through meditation and other forms of mental practices. Costello reminds us that when making an important decision we need to live in the here and now, and not in a past or future.

Besides a rich philosophical amplification, the reader will find in Costello's book solid, practical advice when it comes to actual decision-making: Consider what good does it bring to you and the other; don't decide when you are "lost, lethargic or low"; don't rely on momentary feelings, which is to be distinguished from carpe diem (the imperative of the instant); above all be honest and authentic. Costello brings to our attention the ethical component in decision making. He addresses the need to address the plight of "the minority group, the ostracized, the stranger the widow, the orphan." Costello reminds us to keep in mind, what Jungians call the shadow: Our biases, hidden motivations, and ignorance. When focussing on the final end of life, a spiritual quality of decision-making shines forth: What will be my legacy to the world?

The many lists that the reader encounters in this book are not to be interpreted in terms of factual knowledge, rather as elements that activate or inspire a decision-making process. This process is not simply assessing the externalities of the situation, but, following Jung's notion of

Foreword

the transcendent function, we need to be aware of an inner dialogue between consciousness and the creative unconscious to face the unexpected. Early humankind were aware of this kind of dialogue and invested a lot of energy in creating divination techniques to make the decision-making process more conscious. One the most sophisticated of early divination techniques was the *I Ching*. Costello has written an interesting chapter on the *I Ching* and the *Tarot* and their relevance today, as found in the works of Jung, Progoff, and Valentin Tomberg.

The author ends with a brilliant description of the triune brain, capturing the complexity of the decision-making process in terms of brain-functioning. Even if "the undisputed champion of the triune brain is the reptilian brain," Costello advocates an alignment of all three parts of the brain in the decision-making process. As we execute our choices, we are engaging in a process of creating ourselves to be who we are. I recommend this book to all who wish to know more about the choices they have made and will continue to make as they discover who they are and who they want to become.

John Hill

Introduction

Archimedes Thoughtful, Domenico Fetti, 1620. Public Domain.

DECISIONS ARE FAR TOO important to be left to chance. They impact on virtually every aspect of our lives. We need an approach to decision-making that will enable us to discern well so that we make not only good but great decisions. The aim of this book is to help with precisely that. It sets out the

Introduction

tools necessary for making wise choices. It contains examples and exercises, reflections and practices, questions for consideration, models, and suggestions. The book is both philosophical and practical.

Topics covered in chapter 1 include: the importance of uniting heart (feelings), head (thinking), and hands (doing); a five-step sequence for decision-making; the Law of Three; the Rule of the Last Inch; the five circles of decision; the Stoic fork; a seven-step formula for decision-making; biases and blind-spots; the 4 Rs; Descartes's square; the assets and impediments to decision-making; the four villains of decision-making; and the ego vs the Self. Powerful techniques will be offered so that your choices can be carried out in the light of full knowledge and your decisions enacted with ease and efficiency. Chapter 2 takes the reader through the Enneagram system of personality to adduce how the nine types go about the work of deciding, each with their unique style. We also need to get in touch with our creativity as this will aid the decision-making process as well as our problem-solving capabilities. This dimension will be the focus in chapter 3. Chapter 4 highlights the importance of Theory U to decision-making, while chapter 5 considers synchronicity and how it is the key to unlocking the architectonics of two well-known, so-called divinatory approaches to decision-making—the *I Ching* and Tarot. Finally, chapter 6 gives an account of the triune brain, where I make the point that the so-called reptilian brain is responsible for many of the choices and decisions we make, unbeknownst to ourselves. A postmodern 'PS' on 'undecidability' follows by way of conclusion. A select bibliography is included. There is a thread connecting the content of all the chapters which will become apparent upon reading, one which also links with two other books of mine: *The Nine Faces of Fear* and *Between Speech and Silence* which, taken together, constitute a trilogy of sorts.

1

On Choosing and Deciding

"It is only in our decisions that we are important."—
Jean-Paul Sartre

"Life is a constant process of deciding what we are going to do."—
José Ortega y Gasset

DECISIONS, DECISIONS. CHOICES CONFRONT us daily, demanding action. We muse and mull them over. Choosing requires discriminating which is carried out not by the discursive intellect (what Eastern philosophy calls *manas*, which is the moving mind) but by *buddhi*, the intelligence. A choice is a preference. Sometimes choices paralyze us, making us panic, or procrastinate. They delight or distress us. We become anxious or angry. We hem and we haw, hampered by Hamlet's hesitancy. We dither as we deliberate, sometimes just wishing that it could all be solved with a simple toss of the coin, by chance rather than choice. Heads or tails? Risk versus reward.

> "Excellence is never an accident. It is always the result of high intention, sincere effort, and intelligent execution; it represents the wise choice of many alternatives—choice, not chance, determines your destiny."—Aristotle

> "Decisions, not conditions, determine what a man is."—Viktor Frankl

If *some* choice is good does not necessarily mean that *more* choice is better. Wise choices can be demanding; meanwhile we suffer from the "tyranny of small decisions," as economist Fred Hirsch put it.[1]

Discerning

Discernment is a process leading to a decision. Every choice we make to do one thing entails a decision not to do another thing; there is a yes and a no; there are steppingstones, roads taken and not taken. To discern is to judge well. Discernment is decision-making within a spiritual context. The religious register describes a process of determining God's desire (providence) and is often associated with St. Ignatius of Loyola (1491–1556), founder of the Jesuit Order, who is regarded as a master of discernment and whose *Spiritual Exercises* are concerned with precisely this topic. However, we can recount a story from early on in his career, which he includes in his *Autobiography*, written towards the end of his life, which shows a novice's uncertainty. At this stage in his life, Ignatius had no method for decision-making, no rules for discernment. Like many people, this Spanish-soldier just stumbled along, leaving choices to chance and the Summer breeze.

The Saint and the Donkey

Shortly after his conversion, Ignatius was riding on a donkey on a dusty road in Spain in the company of a Muslim Moor. They were discussing religion and a disagreement ensued. The Moor rode off angrily after imparting some insulting remarks about the Virgin Mary. Ignatius was indignant. He felt it was his knightly duty to defend the honor of Mary by killing the Moor but was not sure if this was consistent with his new-found faith. He left the decision to his donkey. They were approaching a crossroads. If the donkey took the road that the Moor took, Ignatius would follow and kill him. If the donkey took the other road, he would let him go. The donkey took the other road.

Sartre and the Student

> "We are our choices."—Jean-Paul Sartre

---

1. Cited by Schwartz, *Paradox of Choice*, 21.

On Choosing and Deciding

With St. Ignatius, a donkey decided. In ancient Greece, travelers would approach the Oracle at Delphi and put their questions to the Pythia—the high priestesses at the Temple of Apollo. It was hoped that answers here would come from the divine. Most people having to make decisions consult their consciences or their confessors while others seek help from psychotherapists or philosophers. A student once approached Jean-Paul Sartre, the famous twentieth-century French existentialist philosopher, with a dilemma: should he stay at home looking after his frail mother or join the anti-Nazi resistance. In his essay, *Existentialism and Humanism*, Sartre recounts the episode thus:

> As an example, by which you may the better understand this state of abandonment, I will refer to the case of a pupil of mine, who sought me out in the following circumstances. His father was quarrelling with his mother and was also inclined to be a "collaborator"; his elder brother had been killed in the German offensive of 1940 and this young man, with a sentiment somewhat primitive but generous, burned to avenge him. His mother was living alone with him, deeply afflicted by the semi-treason of his father and by the death of her eldest son, and her one consolation was in this young man. But he, at this moment, had the choice between going to England to join the Free French Forces or of staying near his mother and helping her to live. He fully realized that this woman lived only for him and that his disappearance—or perhaps his death—would plunge her into despair. He also realized that, concretely and in fact, every action he performed on his mother's behalf would be sure of effect in the sense of aiding her to live, whereas anything he did in order to go and fight would be an ambiguous action which might vanish like water into sand and serve no purpose. For instance, to set out for England he would have to wait indefinitely in a Spanish camp on the way through Spain; or, on arriving in England or in Algiers he might be put into an office to fill up forms. Consequently, he found himself confronted by two very different modes of action; the one concrete, immediate, but directed towards only one individual; and the other an action addressed to an end infinitely greater, a national collectivity, but for that very reason ambiguous—and it might be frustrated on the way. At the same time, he was hesitating between two kinds of morality; on the one side the morality of sympathy, of personal devotion and, on the other side, a morality of wider scope but of more debatable validity. He had to choose between those two. What could help him to choose? Could the

> Christian doctrine? No. Christian doctrine says: Act with charity, love your neighbor, deny yourself for others, choose the way which is hardest, and so forth. But which is the harder road? To whom does one owe the more brotherly love, the patriot, or the mother? Which is the more useful aim, the general one of fighting in and for the whole community, or the precise aim of helping one particular person to live? Who can give an answer to that a priori? No one. Nor is it given in any ethical scripture. The Kantian ethic says, Never regard another as a means, but always as an end. Very well; if I remain with my mother, I shall be regarding her as the end and not as a means: but by the same token I am in danger of treating as means those who are fighting on my behalf; and the converse is also true, that if I go to the aid of the combatants, I shall be treating them as the end at the risk of treating my mother as a means. If values are uncertain, if they are still too abstract to determine the particular, concrete case under consideration, nothing remains but to trust in our instincts.[2]

Sartre tells him he *is* freedom and must decide for himself. But if he decides to ask for advice from a priest, for example, he still has to decide which priest—the village curate (who will probably tell him to stay at home and look after his mother) or the chaplain at the army barracks (who will probably tell him to fight for France), so he has already made the choice and he seeks the priest out to confirm him in the decision he has already made. This dilemma above is framed in terms of dualism: either-or. But dialectically, the young man could have told his mother that he was going to join the army and informed the army that he was going to look after his mother and then done something else entirely, for example, go into the woods for a picnic (a third way). For Sartre, every choice entails freedom but also anxiety. The refusal to choose (and he gives the example of a woman invited by a man to a restaurant and who has sexual designs for her but the moment he makes explicit his desire by placing his hand on hers, she pretends not to notice—she ignores the moment and just carries on), Sartre terms *mauvaise foi*—bad faith (self-deception). Morally, we must choose.

The Mugger's Choice

Your money or your life? This is no choice at all. Once the choice is offered, you're dead no matter what alternative you take. *To choose is to lose.*

---

2. Sartre, *Existentialism and Humanism*, 35–36.

In choosing one, you lose the other, and because they are interdependent you also lose what you originally chose (for life is the necessary condition for having money, and money is a necessary condition for living). Jacques Lacan, the French psychoanalyst, refuses the limitations of a choice between aporias and prefers a third stance of "inventive sublimation" which involves the win/win formulation of the revolutionary's choice: freedom or death (life without freedom is no life at all).[3] Here, to choose to fight for freedom, to the point of risking all for its sake, is to retain the eternal freedom of a Che Guevara. On the other hand, to choose death rather than forsake one's freedom similarly leaves intact forever the freedom of Socrates who accepted the verdict of the court, despite the unjust charges brought against him, and died after drinking the hemlock.

Viktor Frankl's Hint from Heaven

> "He must decide, for weal or for woe, what will be the monument of his existence." —Viktor Frankl

Professor Viktor Emil Frankl, MD, PhD (1905–1997), the world-renowned Austrian psychiatrist, neurologist, and philosopher, went for a walk one day to ask for, as he put it, a "hint from Heaven." His visa permitted him to leave for America, but he did not want to abandon his elderly parents as he knew their fate would be deportation to a concentration camp. The year was 1941. When he returned to their apartment, he saw a piece of marble lying on the table. His father told him he had found it in the rubble of a burnt down synagogue and that it represented one of the ten commandments. Which one, Viktor eagerly enquired, to which his father retorted: "honor thy father and thy mother so that thy days may be long in the land of the living." Viktor was rooted to the spot. He let the visa lapse and stayed upon the land. Had his prayer been heard? Was it the echo of his unconscious or the voice of his conscience? About such synchronistic events, he would later say in his autobiography, *Recollections*, that he is too ignorant to explain them and too smart to deny them. This Holocaust survivor and Viennese founder of logotherapy and existential analysis did, in fact, live a long life, dying at the age of ninety-two.

> "Man is not 'driven.' Man decides." —Viktor Frankl

3. See Saint-Cyr, "Sublimation in Lacan."

Dynamics of Discernment

"Choices are the hinges of destiny." —Pythagoras

But let us back-track: shortly after he arrived at the Auschwitz railroad station, he was met by Dr. Joseph Mengele, one of the Holocaust's most notorious mass murderers. He was selecting prisoners: to the right for labor in the camps, and to the left for the gas chambers. In Frankl's case, Mengele pointed Frankl's shoulder to the left. But since Frankl recognized no-one in the left line, behind Mengele's back, he switched over to the right line where he had seen a few of his young colleagues. As he put it: "Only God knows where I got that idea or found the courage."[4] Like Frankl, Edith Eger, also a survivor of Auschwitz and author of *The Choice*, realized that choices, however difficult or limited, can even be made within the confines of a concentration camp. In hell, hope can flourish.

"May your choices reflect your *hopes*, not your fears." —Nelson Mandela

Reflection

What has been the most difficult decision you have ever had to make? It is worth giving this question some attention and examine the dynamics involved. In what way was it difficult? What was its effect, impact? How did you come to make the decision?

_____

_____

_____

_____

_____

_____

_____

---

4. Frankl, *Recollections*, 93.

The word "decision" derives from the Latin *decidere* which means "to cut off" or "to cut down." One decision cuts you off from other options. To decide not to decide is also a decision. Disastrous decisions are frequently the result of over-investment by the ego. Inner freedom is the single most important element in decision-making. Think of the image of a scales at equilibrium. One's conscience (which literally means "knowledge with") will guide one. Who knows if this inner compass is not the sound of the Absolute echoing within us? Discernment (from the Latin: *cerno* = to see and *dis-cerno* = "to judge the difference between things") involves coming to see things as they really are in the light of that which is (the created order of being). Thinking about the world as it is not, but might be, is called counterfactual thinking. Day-dreaming and wishful fantasy are the enemies of coming to see the world as it is.

What do you see? What are you looking for? Life is a perpetual pilgrimage in seeing more. Clear or "true vision," as Iris Murdoch once remarked, "occasions right conduct."[5] "Look *here*." Decision-making is practical but it is also eminently philosophical. When we make good decisions, the aftertaste will be sweet rather than sour. Good decision-making takes us out of Plato's cave with its shadows all around, into the light of the sun. They lead us to consolation: *con-sol-ation*, to being-in-the-sun, or abiding, to cite Scripture, in the shade and shelter of the Almighty/Absolute/*Ātman*. Sometimes they lead to a change in mindset—to an attitudinal alteration or adjustment—and other times, to conversion (*metanoia*)—to what Plato calls the *periagoge* or the turning of consciousness in the cave (turning our life around). The movement here is from feeling being hollowed out (secularity) to feeling hallowed (sacrality): from doubt to decisiveness.

Actions

"Act without expectation."—Lao Tzu

"Actions are the doors and windows of being."—Thomas Merton

How should I act? (Immanuel Kant). What is to be done? (Lenin). What do you want most to do with your life? That is the question. How are we to think (head), feel (heart), and act (hands)? Feelings (emotions), thoughts

---

5. Murdoch, *Sovereignty*, 64.

Dynamics of Discernment

(cognitions), and actions form the basis of my daily life. *Five* steps are involved in any endeavor or action *(kriyā)*:

1. Gather together your means of commencing operations.
2. Provide the members (people) and the materials necessary.
3. Distribution of place and time.
4. Counteration of disaster (consider what to do in the event of a disaster).
5. Successful completion.

There are *four* types of action:

1. *Nitya*: obligatory, necessary.
2. *Naimittika*: occasional, special—produced by some particular cause.
3. *Kāmya*: driven by desire.
4. *Nisiddha*: prohibited.

(The last two are said to be prohibited for a person intend on good/spiritually pure and efficacious action).

Examples

In the 1960s African Americans did not obtain full rights through one momentous decision, but through a series of relatively small decisions. One such resolute choice was Rosa Parks's, who decided to take a seat in the front of a bus and make a stand against systemic injustice and racism. Another was taken by two boys, who on seeing someone struggle in a lake, swam out one summer's evening to save a stranger. They felt an inner pull towards more love, greater service, humble self-transcendence. They were daring in the face of danger and daunting odds, demonstrating fearless fortitude. Their decisions revealed something about the point and purpose of their lives. Decision-making is a spiraling circle. The decision is not the goal. The decision is a means to the main purpose of our lives.

Some decisions are influenced by the desire to please or placate others, avoid conflict, be seen to be part of an ingroup, or avoid criticism that stems from an unpopular decision.

On Choosing and Deciding

Exercise

Ask yourself before making a decision: "What's the worst thing that could happen and what I would do about it?"

	Situation	What I would do about it
1.		
2.		
3.		
4.		
5.		
6.		
7.		
8.		
9.		
10.		

We need to be aware of false angels of light; some things may seem good but ultimately reveal themselves to be distractions or disguises for the disgruntled and demanding ego. In the guise of the good, there is something in it for me, some reward, recognition, or recompense. You will find that some heroic deeds seem to take place quickly like a combustion but are usually predated by acts of self-distancing when the person in question has simply observed the course of their thoughts without becoming enmeshed in the whirlwind of the mind. They have sifted through consciousness and ascertained causes and reasons for acting and deciding. They have been on the lookout for false sentimentality and seductive fantasy. The witness Self (*Säksin*) simply observes the colors and contours of thoughts and feelings; it does not perform any actions. The mind and body are instruments of the Absolute. The important thing is to stay in

Dynamics of Discernment

the present and meet the meaning of the moment, the need of the hour, discerning in stillness the decision that requires attention. St. Ignatius would advise that we make ourselves indifferent to all created things (be interiorly free), that we consider instead only the end for which I have been created. We can put it in another way: do not sweat the small stuff. What is it you seek? For what are you grateful? The first precondition is to get quiet, to still the mind, the inner chatterbox. It is not possible to quieten oneself amid a cacophony of competing values and voices clamoring for attention. Conviction and clarity will emerge only from calm. This will show itself as the midway between an excess and a deficiency, between a hasty (rushing) and hesitant (ruminating) decision.

Detaching from Disordered Desire

Dispose oneself for availability to the Other; surrender personal preferences; ground decision-making in indifference (unattached to outcome), free from disordered desire through detaching from a result. Here we can distance from the desired outcome. We can, as Rainer Maria Rilke put it, "love the questions themselves"—love and live our questions.[6] Discernment is never a choice between good and evil nor is it decoding secret signals. It is about realizing our true nature and acting from that knowledge. Discernment is dynamic and can be dramatic. It is about attunement to the Self, alignment with the Absolute (Ātman). This is just one way of describing it. This being in sync with the (higher/truer/deeper) Self brings us from perturbation to peace and lends a stillness to all our decision making. Becoming more aware—paying attention—necessarily moves us from a place of reaction (instincts) to response (reason). The signs of a good decision include freedom, engagement of the whole person—body, mind, and heart—and deeper knowledge of the Self: the trajectory is from an "I"-thought to "I-I" (Self-awareness—indeed, the Self is awareness). Good decisions bring balance, wholeness. They are about depth not destination, growth not goals. The process will involve the unity of head, heart, and hands, of thinking, feeling, and doing.

- Head: cognition — awareness
- Heart: commitment — appreciation
- Hand: correspondence — action

6. Rilke, *Letters*, 27.

Two Types of Decisions

From the very outset, we need to distinguish between *superficial* and *serious* decisions. An example of the former would be: "should I bus or bike into work this morning?" It is the region of the mundane and the everyday—the empirical or relative. The second category is far deeper and concerns justice, truth, goodness, etc.—this is the realm of the absolute or ultimate. If the first is practical, the second is philosophical. The little decisions can be carried out with one's ego (*ahāmkara*) but for the large decisions one needs to co-opt the Self.

The advice in relation to the first would be just to *get on with it*. For those who are prone to procrastination (especially Nines on the Enneagram), we can suggest: *padam, padam* or "step by step" as a rule to follow. *Päda* is Sanskrit for "foot" (Latin: *pes*), with derived meanings of "stepping" or "striding." As a measure of length, a *pada* amounts to 12 or 15 fingers' breadth. So, proceed one step at a time.

We can decide 1) not to go with our habitual ways of proceeding, and 2) we can develop a love for what is truer, finer, more glorious. Our big decisions can reflect to what we are giving our attention.

A Five-Step Process

The following is the right order of the organized, deciding person. He/she will follow a *five*-step sequence:

Goal → Plan → Desire → Confidence → Determination

Most people begin with planning, without having a clear goal, i.e., a set of clear objectives. So, do not start with the plan; begin with the goal. The plan will arise out of the goal. Plans proliferate and the *manas* (moving) mind can get sucked into them. Goals can be either short or long-term.

> "Man is a goal-setting animal. His life only has meaning
> if he is reaching and striving for his goals."—Aristotle

> "Life can be pulled by goals just as it can be pushed by drives."—
> Viktor Frankl

Dynamics of Discernment

So, think of a decision you have to make, and let it pass through the five-step sequence above:

1. Goal _____

2. Plan _____

3. Desire _____

4. Confidence _____

5. Determination _____

The Law of Three

Now, in relation to more serious decisions pertaining to the purpose of one's being and the nature of creation, the condition most conducive to that type of decision-making is stillness of the mind. The most potent action arises from such deep stillness. We can distinguish *three* aspects to every action:

- *Creative*: the importance of impulse and intention
- *Sustaining*: the greatest power of action comes from love (then discipline and duty, which can grow into love)
- *Dissolving*: the need for patience and perseverance to avoid the sting in the tail

Or we can describe the law of three that governs every action thus:

- Positive (+)
- Negative (-)
- Neutralizing (=)

To every action there is always a reaction, but we must then transcend this dichotomy. The third way is the exit from opposition. These *three* forces are always present. For example, when speaking, you have two people and the listening/talking that takes place between them. In physics, we might mention subatomic particles carrying three charges:

- Proton: positive
- Electron: negative
- Neutron: neutral

We can see this interplay with the three gunah of *sattva*, *rajas*, and *tamas*, which is a veritable forcefield of energy:

- Sattva: harmonious/goodness; gives light, knowledge, and wellbeing—*constructive*
- Rajas: active/passion; gives movement, creativity, and enthusiasm—*confused*
- Tamas: dark/destructive; gives rest, regulation and brings dissolution—*chaotic*

Stillness in the being produces the guna of sattvica energy which leads us from stillness into resoluteness and action. *Buddhi* is the faculty of mind which reasons and judges, understands, discriminates, discerns, decides. It is derived from the Sanskrit root *Budh* meaning "to wake, attend, observe, be conscious of." The energy at play here is different from the *manas* mind which is ever changing. If *manas* relates to the world of the senses (becoming), *buddhi* applies to the world of reason/truth (being). And it is *buddhi* which is required in order to ascertain the differences between what is just and unjust, truth and falsehood, being and becoming. If *manas* learns as it goes, *buddhi* is innate and present from the beginning. Where *manas* is concerned with busyness, *buddhi* connects us with stillness and the Self. When the ego sees itself as the sole source of action, its agency is limited. In meditation, we are able to draw on the rich resources/energy system of the luminous Self.

So, before a big decision, sit in silence for, say, twenty to thirty minutes. Observe what arises in the being when sattvica energy is deployed. Then become aware, especially, if you feel boxed in by a dualistic decision, in other words, this or that, right or wrong, either-or, of the third dimension beyond this conflictual dichotomy. Look for the "third space."

Dynamics of Discernment

The Rule of the Last Inch

When we decide on a course of action, it is important to obey what Russian writer Aleksandr Solzhenitsyn described as "the rule of the last inch" in his novel, *The First Circle*, which states that:

1. we should not leave anything undone
2. neither should we put it off
3. nor should we try to complete the activity as soon as possible but rather to bring it to perfection

He writes:

> Now, listen to the rule of the last inch. The realms of the last inch. The job is almost finished, the goal almost attained; everything possible seems to have been achieved, every difficulty overcome—and yet the quality is just not there. The work needs more finish, ... In that moment of weariness and self-satisfaction, the temptation is greatest to give up, not to strive for the peak of quality. That is the realm of the last inch—here, the work is very complex, but it is also particularly valuable because it's done with the most perfect means. The rule of the last inch is simply this—not to leave it undone. And not to put it off—because otherwise your mind loses touch with that realm. And not to mind how much time you spend on it, because the aim is not to finish the job quickly, but to reach perfection.[7]

The Rule of the Last Inch is the full completion of an action. We allow the action to be dissolved into stillness until it leaves no residue, and we surrender all claims upon it. We deliver it/send it out into the universe. Do you apply the Rule of the Last Inch to your work?

Five Circles

We frequently begin making decisions from the perspective and position of the personal but ethical decisions go out into, and have ramifications for, the whole wide world. We can adduce *five* concentric circles:

- Me
- Family

---

7. Solzhenitsyn, *First Circle*, 183–84.

- Society
- Humanity
- World

Thought, decision, love, and will are universal powers. The *Ātman* or Self is the owner of these powers. We need to observe the effect of *sattva*, *rajas*, and *tamas* on the will, because these gunah will render the will constant, fickle, or obdurate. The will needs to be based on reason. When the intellect understands the true nature of creation, it is sattvic. When the intellect does not understand what is right and wrong, and what should be done and what not, it is under the sway of *rajas*. And that which, shrouded in ignorance, thinks wrong right, that intellect is ruled by *tamas* (see the *Bhagavad Gita*, chapter 18, verse 30–32). When the action is good, the outcome is auspicious. A bad action done in the dark produces harmful effects. So, see the effects your decision will have in terms of the circles of concern outside yourself.

Techniques

The good news is that there are tried and tested tools and techniques for making good decisions, guidelines governing decision-making, so that we do not have to leave everything to cruel and capricious fate (*fortuna*). Choice is about freedom, and decisions are about desires—about what we want and who we are.

Advice

We may look for signs—cues, clues—but not miracles. Or we may imagine that we are on our death-bed- looking back over our lives in order to arrive at a detached decision. You can carry out this exercise now—just look back over your life and see the effect your decisions and choices have had. We may look to what we really want from life. Our deepest desire is the Self's deepest desire. We are pulled and pushed, driven, and drawn. Our decisions take place in the field of pull and counter-pull, as Plato recognized. He described the person (as a puppet of the gods) being drawn up to the divine realm and being dragged down to the underworld. It is important to discover the Golden Thread that *draws* us rather than follow the direction of the steely cord that *drags* us down to Hades and possibly to

Dynamics of Discernment

Tartarus—the place of punishment (though as C. S. Lewis once remarked, "the doors to hell are locked on the inside."[8] We are punished *by* our sins not *for* our sins). So, try to apply these three to your decisions. Enquire: "am I . . . by my decisions"?

- Dragged
- Driven
- Drawn

If we wish to avoid obvious "evil," the choice is between two goods. The question then arises: what is the best way to proceed? One important instruction we need to make at the outset is this: to try to live in the here and now when making a decision, and not be in the past or future. It is important to stay in the present reality (to be without memory or desire). Be suspicious of the urgent—in other words, take time when deciding. Do not let yourself be rushed. It is important to get perspective, set priorities, and not be put under any undue pressure. One should not decide anything when in an agitated, anxious, or angry state. Let the emotions subside.

> "When you are angry, it is better to postpone the decision."—Seneca

Be honest with yourself. Identify patterns. Recognize biases, blind-spots, blockages. Consult with others (a spiritual director, philosopher, priest, pastor, or psychotherapist). Self-distance: enquire as to what advice you would give to someone else in the same situation. Do not feel trapped—there are always choices to be made. You are free to choose how to respond to situations. Integrate head (thinking), heart (feeling), and hand (journaling) in any decision (holistic discernment). Your whole being makes a decision—intellect, emotions, intuition, imagination etc. Ask: what is the need here? What is the greatest good for others? Look at your talents/gifts and not just at your achievements/accomplishments. Write them down. Do not make decisions when you are feeling lost, lethargic, or low. Permanent decisions should not be made on the basis of temporary feelings.

> "A good decision is based on knowledge and not on numbers."—Plato

Pay attention to where you are being led in terms of consolation or desolation. Try a decision on for size. Sift through your consciousness to decide

---

8. Lewis, *Problem of Pain*, 130.

wisely and well. Gather/garnish all the information you can. Weigh up the alternatives. Be objective; do not personalize through partisanship, personalized preferences, or projections. Remember: there is no such thing as a right or wrong decision—only good or bad ones. It is better to be honest than to be right.

> "In any moment of decision, the best thing you can do is the right thing. The worst thing you can do is nothing."—Theodore Roosevelt

Seek confirmation—serenity or a sense of purpose—a confirmation, consolidation, consolation or prefigurement of completion. Commit to a decision once made. Make the decision in good faith, for all things work to the good. Few decisions are irrevocable.

> "Concision in style, precision in thought, decision in life."—Victor Hugo

Exercise

First a question: How would you say you normally make decisions? Now, get a sheet of paper or notepad and write on a page the decisions you have made. List your *macro* decisions, for example, to marry, move to a new house, change jobs, and your *micro* decisions—these matter too, as they form attitudes—how I treat others, my prejudices, how I spend my time, money, talents. Whatever you fall in love with determines everything really. Love itself is a decision.

Macro Decisions

_____

_____

_____

_____

_____

Dynamics of Discernment

Micro Decisions

_____

_____

_____

_____

I make choices in regard to all I actively do, but also in relation to what happens to me passively—to the things I cannot avoid such as birth, culture, family, accidents, global events, sickness, ageing, dying. I can, of course, decide how I respond to these. There is a Stoic exercise.

The Stoic Fork: A Dichotomy of Control

Draw *two* circles or make two columns. Put in the first circle all the things you can control/change/create and in the second circle name all the things outside your control.

Things I Can Control

_____

_____

_____

_____

_____

Things I Cannot Control

_____

_____

_____

_____

_____

You will see that all you can really control is your attitude/mindset and actions. Everyone else's behavior is outside our control. In your attitude, you are free. We are bound in every aspect except in *bahavana* (Sanskrit for "attitude").

> "Some things are in our control, others are not." —Epictetus

> "Everything can be taken from a man but one thing: the last of the human freedoms—to choose one's attitude in any given set of circumstances, to choose one's own way." —Viktor Frankl

"The Serenity Prayer" by Reinhold Niebuhr captures the above sentiments well:

> God grant me the serenity
> to accept the things I cannot change;
> courage to change the things I can;
> and wisdom to know the difference.[9]

The Bigger Questions

We find ourselves in life, on stage, besieged and bombarded with choices of every color and stripe, with decisions of every kind. Some seek answers in prayer, believing in a benevolent Providence at work in the world, which

---

9. "The Serenity Prayer," by Reinhold Niebuhr (1892–1971), composed in 1932–1933. Adopted by Alcoholics Anonymous. Appears in a sermon by Niebuhr in 1944.

possesses the contours of a game-plan rather than the structure of an architect's drawing. We are confronted with freedom, both essential and effective. We may listen to our conscience, our inner moral compass, our ethical intuition, our interior space where we hearken in silence and secret to the still, small voice. We need to find out who we want to be and what sort of life we want to lead. A life of meaning or money? (One does not preclude the other; indeed, the latter often comes as a by-product or side-effect of the former). What do you want to do with your wild and wonderful life? We need to find and fulfil our unique task—some definite service. What do you think yours is? How often do you consult your conscience, check in with your moral compass before making a decision?

> "Everyone has his own specific vocation or mission in life; everyone must carry out a concrete assignment that demands fulfilment. Therein he cannot be replaced, nor can his life be repeated. Thus, everyone's task is unique as is his specific opportunity to implement it."—Viktor Frankl

Our inner freedom is critical/crucial. Both Sartre and Frankl felt free in a concentration camp. We need to choose the wisest and most loving options. Good decision-making is complex: it involves instinct, emotion, reason, knowledge, conscience, desire, good judgement, practical wisdom—they all play their part. And it is not just about us. How do my choices impact on my family and friends, even my country? "Who speaks for Wolf?"—the Other—the excluded, the member of the minority group, the ostracized, the stranger, the widow, the orphan? Communal discernment is important too—a group think-tank rather than groupthink, a consultative process involving key stakeholders.

I need to notice patterns in my behavior, check my biases, discern my motivations. I can enquire: Do I know all the facts? Have I taken time to research? Do I listen to others? Have I weighed up the pros and cons: for and against? Have I listened to the heart's promptings—to the movements of attraction and aversion? The conviction that you did your best (rather than being certain) is enough. We can set out a *seven*-step sequence thus:

Seven Steps in Decision-Making

1. Seek spiritual freedom—the inner disposition upon which discernment rests.
2. Name the choice or issue you face. What is really at stake?
3. Evaluate the appropriate data.
4. Reflect. Pause.
5. Formulate a tentative decision.
6. Seek confirmation—the sense you are on the right track.
7. Assess the process—are there any parts that are filled with anxiety?

Become aware of feelings (existential moods) of *consolation*: confidence, courage, epiphany, peace, conviction, harmony, liberation, desire to serve others; and of *desolation*: empty and meaningless (what Frankl calls the "existential vacuum"), rumination and worry, being at odds with oneself and out of sync, fearful and forlorn, recalcitrant, and reluctant, revolted. There are *three* layers/levels of affectivity, which we may visualize as *three* concentric circles: the crust, the mantle, and the core of the earth. The first circle is the outer one. This contains my most immediate impressions, my most spontaneous instinctive reactions. Here, the feelings appear and disappear quickly (e.g., the leap from laughter to tears). Suffice to say, we cannot make decisions at this level of affective unpredictability. If we do, we will be like flotsam and jetsam—at the mercy of constantly changing currents in the world of becoming. The middle layer is what we might call emotion or feeling—they are more profound than the superficial ones on the outer level. The third level is the center, the soul, the core. This receptive silent space within produces feelings of clarity and certainty. This is the area of real choice, as it is the area of real freedom. Here we are liberated from being lackeys, as we have found the still point of the fulcrum. And we waste no time wavering. We do not decide from a place of wounds or weakness but interior freedom (*moksha*).

"I am forever returning to the still center."—Iris Murdoch

Discernment is an instrument of struggle. It is not a form of egotistical introspection.

We are always enjoined not to make decisions hastily—they require patience, waiting. We should attempt to see the dilemma from other points of view. There will always be an element of surprise, an area of uncertainty, and unpredictability.

Decision-Making Wisdom

- We all have an inner Sat-Nav which can guide us to our true Self. Trust it.
- Ask: does this satisfy me deep down or am I just doing it to please or placate others?
- Remember: we cannot have it every way. To say "yes" to one thing means saying "no" to another. Every "positive" choice has a "negative" underside.
- Let the thoughts and feelings settle and reach a point of calm: let the decision be attuned to one's heart-core. Bring your head and heart together.
- Seek out sound advice: Listen to people who know you well. They can help you to clarify what you want.
- To make good decisions, learn to be attentive.
- In making a decision, it is good to have a realistic alternative choice against which you can measure your proposed decision.
- What decision gives me inner peace, what decision do I most deeply want? What decision draws more on my talents? What decision makes more rational sense? What decision will lead to better service of others?
- Form at least two possible outcomes in your mind.
- Take account of the concrete context of the situation. What are the needs here? How can I best meet them? How can I make a difference? Take a look at the challenges surrounding the choice.
- We need to come to know ourselves: How have I been gifted? What do I most love doing? At what do I excel? What are my strengths and weaknesses? Ask others: do they confirm what I see in myself?
- Dare to dream the Big Picture. What are you passionate about? What really excites, energizes, and enlivens you? Mull over your dreams and desires.

On Choosing and Deciding

- Talents: write down what you think your talents are. Look for your gifts and not just your achievements.
- Feelings: pay attention to your feelings, both negative and positive, those that drive and those that draw you.
- Do not make a decision in times of desolation.
- Be aware of your tendency to procrastinate, to put off, and rationalize—convinced that your personal preference is the right one.

"Man is lost by indecision than wrong decision. Indecision is the thief of opportunity. It will steal you blind."—Cicero

- Use your imagination—it opens up possible worlds of meaning.
- From two alternatives take the first one and imagine yourself occupying that choice as if you were living it right now. Step into that choice—make it your own. Notice how you are feeling. Do you feel at home in it or not? Does it fit with your gifts? What is the experience like? Then step into the second choice and go through the same process from the other perspective. Experience the choice as a lived reality.

"Good decisions come from experience. Experience comes from making bad decisions."—Mark Twain

Compare and contrast the two experiences—which one appeals to your deep Self?

- Commit. Be resolute. The time for deliberation is over. There will always be unforeseen consequences.

The "will" deliberates over decisions, just as it is the task of *phronesis* or practical wisdom to actually make meaningful decisions. A number of mechanisms have been put forward to guide people in their decision-making. We will list *two* of them below. They may help, but it is important not to reduce these decisional balance-sheets to a mechanics and mathematics of accountancy.

Dynamics of Discernment

GOFER

Psychologist Leon Mann and his colleagues developed **GOFER** in the 1980s. It is an acronym for decision-making steps originally taught to adolescents.[10]

    Goals: survey values and objectives

    Options: consider the range of alternative options

    Facts: search for information

    Effects: weigh the pros and cons, the positive and negative consequences

    Review: plan how to implement the options

DECIDE

In 2008, Kristina Guo created the six-step sequence **DECIDE**:[11]

    Define the problem

    Establish/enumerate the criteria/constraints

    Consider/collect all the alternatives

    Identify the best alternatives

    Develop a plan of action and implement it

    Evaluate the selection. Examine feedback if necessary.

Biases and Blind spots

Avoid analysis-paralysis; hyper-reflection leads to procrastination. Delimit desires (Epicurus). Possible personal biases include:

- Confirmation bias: the selective search for evidence that supports certain conclusions while disregarding other facts.
- Cognitive inertia: the unwillingness to change existing thought patterns in the light of new circumstances.

---

10. Mann et al., "Effectiveness of the GOFER Course."
11. Guo, "DECIDE."

- Selective perception: actively screening out information deemed to be unimportant.
- Wishful thinking: the tendency to want to see things in a certain—usually positive—light which can distort perception and thinking.
- Groupthink: peer pressure to conform to the opinions held by a particular group.
- Optimism bias: overestimating the likelihood of positive events and underestimating the likelihood of negative life-events.

Be on the lookout for these in your decision-making.

A Three-Stage Sequence

We can map the phases in any decision-making process thus:

1. Need—decision
2. Decision—resolution
3. Resolution—action

The big decisions take place against the backdrop of the purpose of my life. Much will depend on how I see my nature as a human being, on the essential nature of creation, and whether I am motivated by profit, pleasure, peace, or purpose. Am I trying to accept or resist my life and the events therein? What sort of a person do I wish to be, and to be remembered as? What will be written on my tombstone? What am I going to contribute to the world—what will my legacy be? Wherein lies my happiness—within or without? What will I do in terms of my work ("love made visible") in the world and how will I choose it?

If you do not know your purpose, shouldn't you take time to enquire about it? Everything has a purpose. Clocks tell time and trains take you places. What is your life-plan/project? Pay attention to your thoughts and feelings—they are indicators. When you pause, you will begin to notice what you are thinking and how you are feeling—these will tell you something about yourself. Only when you are peace can you make a decision prudently. Feelings can mislead, so it is important to pay attention to them day after day, situation after singular situation. What charges you with delight and what depletes or depresses you? What grips you with gratitude? Gratitude, to paraphrase G. K. Chesterton, is happiness magnified by marvel (wonder). What bids you break and what inspires you, igniting heroic action? Does what you do engender joy, bliss, or boundless delight (*ananda*)? We can pause to ponder these existential questions thus, by choosing to engage with one or more of the following *five*.

Five Practices

- *Lectio*: reading the words of the wise (for example, Scriptures)
- *Consideratio*: contemplating things by comparing them (inspecting them from various perspectives)
- *Oratio*: praying
- *Meditatio*: meditating
- *Discernimento*: judging and deciding

Trust your experience. This is the arena for discernment. Thoughtful reflection demonstrates the direction we should take in our work in the world. Life is an ongoing process of discernment—a call within a call. Look for happiness and joy rather than just pleasure, which is fleeting. Joy is deep desire. Happiness is our birth-right—do not let it be burgled. Our talents (innate) and skills (learned) permit us to play our role in the drama of creation. Ask:

- What skills do I have?
- What talents do I have?
- What am I good at?
- What do I have a knack for?

Three Contexts

St Ignatius of Loyola felt that decisions were made in *three* circumstances:

1. When there is no doubt—here the decision is crystal clear.
2. When feelings are unsettled—here our emotions are in turmoil, from fear to confusion. The advice here is not to make a decision against the backdrop of desolation. We need to move from reaction to response,

and observe and interpret our feelings, to discern and discover their spiritual meaning.

3. When emotions are calm—here we decide in a circumstance and context of calm which is conducive to weighing the pros and cons.

Of course, our life changes, or rather, our variable states change. We may give here an analogy of the various states of materials. Metal and plastic are solid states, but they can be melted. When frozen, they are solid. If the temperature rises, they will become liquid. It now is water and has a different function. The water might become a gas or become solid ice cubes. *Our state changes, but our essential Self remains.* A cup and a vase are still clay—they just have different functions. We need to discern our various mutable states.

Listen to your heart (Max Scheler: "the order of the heart").[12] *Chitta* is the emotional ground of being. We talk about the "heart of the matter," in other words, the center or core. This can guide us. Deep calls unto deep. What stirs within you? We need to become attuned to our body's feelings as much as our "felt sense." Ignatius asks that we try on a decision, and test each option out (acting "as-if"). Live as if we have already made the decision and see where that leads you.

Four Levels of Consciousness

According to Jesuit philosopher-theologian, Bernard Lonergan, there are *four* levels of waking consciousness: experience, understanding, judging, and deciding.[13] In relation to deciding, we have reached the region of freedom and responsibility, of moral self-transcendence, of self-direction in our bid to make responsible decisions.

1. Sensual experience (empirical)
2. Understanding (intellectual)
3. Judgement/reflection (rational)
4. Application (responsible)

---

12. Scheler, "*Ordo Amoris.*"
13. Lonergan, *Insight*, 27.

Dynamics of Discernment

So, after experiencing, understanding, judging, we need to decide. This is how we grow in discernment and decision-making. He exhorts us to be *five* things.

Five Be-attitudes

1. Be attentive
2. Be intelligent
3. Be reasonable
4. Be responsible
5. Be loving

These all contribute to our being decisive. We experience our deciding; we understand our deciding; we affirm the reality of our deciding; we decide to operate in accord with the norms immanent in the relatedness of our experienced, understood, understanding, judging, and deciding. The aim: to heighten our consciousness of deliberating and deciding. We decide for weal or for woe what the meaning of our life will be; we decide who we are and what we want. It is about our outlook, horizon, worldview. Such a deliberate desire is authentic rather than arbitrary. It is total surrender, as Lonergan puts it, to the demands of the human spirit, that we be attentive, intelligent, reasonable, responsible, loving—and decisive. It should not, he contends, be conceived as an act of the will (this is old-fashioned faculty psychology). Decision-making pertains to the realm of the free and the responsible. It is the work, not of a will, but of conscience and conversion. To help with this process, we can fill in *four* columns.

The Four Columns Exercise

I will accept the		I will NOT accept the	
(e.g., teaching post in London)		(e.g., teaching post in London)	
Advantages to Me/us	Disadvantages to me/us	Advantages to me/us	Disadvantages to me/us

Important and Urgent Decisions

"The most urgent decisions are rarely the most important ones." — Dwight Eisenhower

Important, not urgent
Decide when you will do it

Urgent and important
Do it immediately

Not important, not urgent
Do it later

Urgent, not important
Delegate to someone else

We need to balance cost and time. Whenever you've an important decision to make, write down what you expect will happen. Compare your expectation later with the actual outcome.

Expectation   Result

The bigger the overlap between the two, the better you will be at evaluating. Remember this anagram: **KISS: K**eep **I**t **S**imple, **S**tupid. (Simple, but no simpler, as Einstein remarked). Utilize the "rubber band model": what is holding me back? What is pulling/propelling me forward?

Feedback analysis

Ask for feedback, of which there are *four* forms:

1. Advice
2. Compliment
3. Criticism
4. Suggestion

And beware of the choice overload. Choices can confuse. More is difficult.

10-10-10 Technique

What consequences will my decisions have in:

- 10 days?
- 10 months?

Dynamics of Discernment

- 10 years?

Flow

Look for the happiness you experience when engaged in something meaningful that you love, which absorbs all your attention. You are said to be in a state of "flow." This occurs when we are:

- Focused on an activity
- of our own choosing, that is
- neither under-challenging (boredom) or over-challenging (burnout), that has
- a clear objective which receives
- immediate feedback.

Knowns and Unknowns

Sometimes our actions may not be consistent with our beliefs, in which cases cognitive dissonance ensues. We need to take into account of:

1. Knowns
2. Unknowns

1. Known knowns
2. Known unknowns
3. Unknown knowns
4. Unknown unknowns

Conflict Situations

Decisions, especially when involving others, can lead to conflict. We can deal with this in *six* main ways:

1. Flight: lose-lose
2. Fight: win-lose

3. Give up: lose-win
4. Evade responsibility: lose-lose
5. Compromise: win-lose; lose-win
6. Reach a consensus: win-win (the third way)

Pictograms

We may wish to draw a mind-map or pictogram which acts as a visual aid to our decision-making. For example:

- Iceberg: draws attention to a growing or upcoming problem
- Temple: illustrates success
- Bridge: shows connection
- Conveyor belt: demonstrates procedures and processes
- Funnel: consolidates ideas
- Pyramid: denotes hierarchy

Circling

We can perambulate around the problem. What are the facts? What are my feelings about the facts? What are my thoughts? Ask: what, why, how, where, when, and so what? Distinguish between the important the incidental, the urgent and the unnecessary. Check your presumptions. Suspend your presuppositions, prejudices, and projections. Be aware of your biases and blind spots, your assumptions, attractions, aversions, and attachments. This is what we have been saying.

We can:

- Brainstorm possible solutions.
- State the solution clearly as a positive statement followed by its contrary.
- Set up the four-column method above for each double statement.

Dynamics of Discernment

The Three Times When a Good Choice May be Made

1. First time: when the will is moved or attracted.
2. Second time: when we receive the light from above through the experience of consolation and desolation and discernment of diverse spirits.
3. Third time: this is a time of tranquility—when the soul is not agitated by different spirits.

We should seek confirmation in this third time. Consolation is the true touchstone for correctly discerning a decision, according to Ignatius. We can carry this out in detail during the recommended daily Ignatian examen, when we sit quietly for fifteen minutes at the beginning and end of each day, sifting through the events, the choices and decisions I have made, the encounters and episodes of the day, enquiring:

- What have I done?
- What have I left undone?
- If I had the time over, what would I do differently?

Aids

- Imagine yourself giving advice to another person
- Imagine yourself on your death-bed
- Try it on for size

Try to practice Ignatian "indifference"—this consists in detaching from the desired outcome. Detachment (non-attachment) is the first step in discernment. It is also recommended by mediaeval mystic Meister Eckhart and the Buddha, as well as Advaita Vedanta in Indian philosophy. Delimit desires. Hold the desire for something along with a sense of inner freedom with respect to the same thing. Desire without possession. These *three* terms are synonymous: detachment: disidentification: indifference. This kind of indifference is inner freedom, is grace—it's not a callous "I couldn't care less".

The examen involves an existential election: instead of asking "what am I getting from this transaction," ask "what am I giving?" And "what is this decision freeing me *from* and freeing me *for*?" Our elections should be made in the light of self-emptying (*kenosis*), of self-transcendence. Awareness/attention leads to action: Be clear about the end you seek, the purpose of your choice. Ask: what are you seeking? What is it you want?

You can be analytical: choosing between two goods by listing pros and cons in two columns—what Ignatius calls a "third-time" choice, or we can be guided by your heart ("first-time" and "second-time" choices), where we discern less from our reasoning intellect and more from the movements and meanings of our emotions—the reasoning heart. Philosopher Blaise Pascal: "the heart has its reasons of which reason knows nothing." Or we can plunge into almost immediate action without too much thought being expended. How we make decisions is dependent, to some extent, on how we see the world, whether it be coherent, capricious, or cruel. There is the rational choice model—man understood as a rational animal (Aristotle) capable of making decisions logically (Leibnitz: "Let us calculate").[14] There is the gut-instinct model—where we make decisions on the intuitive level. There is some sort of combination—between heart and head, emotions, and intellect.

Saying No with Love

Philosopher-novelist Iris Murdoch once suggested "falling out of love" can allow for "new eneriges as a result of refocusing."[15] Stop seeing certain people. Stop going to certain places. Walking away or saying no with love might be the answer. So, it is not always about "saying yes to life in spite of everything."[16] Sometimes it is about saying no. Economists distinguish about the *sunk cost* (the past—the time or money or long hours you have put into someone or something) and *opportunity cost* (the future: for every hour you have spent on one thing, you are giving up the opportunity to spend that hour on something else). If only we were not so worried about the sunk cost, we may just be able to walk away, to "consent to distance," in the words of philosopher Simone Weil.

Life is constant course-correction. Do not be afraid of failing. As Samuel Beckett put it: fail again, fail better! Einstein: "Anyone who has never made a mistake has never tried anything new." We can outline *eight* steps.

---

14. This phrase appears in several places in Leibnitz's writing. See Leibnitz, *New Essays*.

15. Murdoch, "On 'God,'" 345.

16. See Frankl, *Yes to Life*.

Dynamics of Discernment

Eight Steps

1. Identify the decision to be made. The issue to be resolved should be practical, real. You have got to have the necessary information to decide intelligently. You could:
   a. List the upcoming decisions.
   b. List the actions you might take about these issues.
   c. List the pros and cons for each issue or possible action.
   d. Rank the issues in terms of preference.
   e. Focus on that list in order.

2. Formulate the issue in a proposal,
   a. state it as a positive concrete choice,
   b. make it specific,
   c. state it in the form of X vs non-X or X vs Y.
   d. Do a **SWOT** analysis—identifying **s**trengths, **w**eaknesses, **o**pportunities, **t**hreats.
   e. Discuss it with a wise man/woman,
   f. Understand the possible obstacles: projections, disordered attachments, complexes, fear, past hurt, desire for power or status etc.

3. Gather all the necessary information—inform your choice as much as your conscience. Ask who, what, where, when, how much, why etc.

4. Consult. Get input.

5. State the reasons for and against each alternative.

   Stay in Ireland (example)

   Advantages for me   Disadvantages for me

   1. _____   1. _____

   2. _____   2. _____

   3. _____   3. _____

Go to London:

Advantages for me	Disadvantages for me
1. _____	1. _____
2. _____	2. _____
3. _____	3. _____

6. Do a formal evaluation of the all the advantages and disadvantages—get in contact with your motives and values.
7. Observe the direction of your will—notice how your will becomes more inclined toward one option and less inclined to another.
8. Attend to experiences of consolation about the preferred option, to joy, hope, love, courage, confidence etc. Ask: where is the movement coming from and where is it leading me? Just as spiritual consolation does not always mean happiness, neither does spiritual desolation equate to sadness. Suffering can be a moment of grace.

The 4 Rs

1. Review: being mindful
2. Rest and reflect: get away
3. Return: to work
4. Repeat: return to activity

Decisions can be derailed by unconscious factors. Emotions can often hijack rational thought (David Hume: "reason is and ought to be only the slave of the passions and can pretend to no other office other than to serve and obey them.")[17] But that does not mean we should solely go on gut instinct. We need to integrate heart and head. As opposed to the Cartesian split/rift (deriving from Descartes), the Greeks always emphasized integration and synthesis. The emotional ground of our being can work in sync with our minds. Emotional regulation bids us to think of decisions in terms of a complex self in a complex world. (Freud had offered a tripartite model of id which "wants," of an ego which "can," and of a superego which "should").

---

17. Hume, *Treatise*, 415.

Dynamics of Discernment

If we could develop our moral sentiments, we could trust our decision-making abilities in just about any situation. Freud: "The normal man is not only far more immoral than he believes but also far more moral than he any idea of."[18] We need to nurture the better angels of our nature—*logos, nous*.

There may seem to be only two options available: the rational choice model (logical decision-making) or the gut instinct model (intuitive feeling) but we can combine them, as we said. The Chinese have a word: *xin* to denote "mind-heart." (C. G. Jung was once told by Pueblo Indians that they think with the heart.)[19] Cultivating the heart-mind is what fosters our ability to decide wisely and well. Good decisions do not just come from feeling or reasoning but from a complete understanding of what our heart-mind knows is the right thing to do, when the cognitive and the connotative are integrated and oriented to the true, the good and the beautiful, and ordered to meaning. *We can use our mind to cultivate our emotions.* In this context, we need to become aware of all the triggers and old patterns of behavior; thus, the importance and imperative of refining our responses. We need to work with what is in front of us, with the need that appears. As Epictetus reminds us: "Do not wish to have things happen as you wish them to happen but to happen as they do happen and you will be happy"—acceptance and self-surrender, which does not necessarily mean approval. Things will happen that we cannot control but we have a choice to act. The world is a shifting not stable place, and an infinite array of possibilities present themselves to us and it is this complexity that we must honor.

Descartes's Square

René Descartes (1596–1650) was one of the founders of modern philosophy. He was also an engineer and mathematician. He is best known for his statement *cogito, ergo sum* (*Je pense, donc Je suis*): "I think, therefore I am." He laid the foundations for 17th-century Continental rationalism.

Descartes's model—the Square—allows us to understand the consequences of any choice. It is designed to make us think and record everything down—a guide that guarantees a good decision gets made. It is based on *four* simple, practical questions, which can be applied in everyday life.

Instructions

18. Freud, *The Ego and the Id*, 48.
19. Jung, *Memories*, 248.

Divide your paper into four squares, with one question in each and start answering these questions according to your problem. Thus:

- What will happen if this happens? (top left)
- What will happen if this doesn't happen? (top right)
- What won't happen if this happens? (bottom left)
- What won't happen if this doesn't happen? (bottom right)

Example

What if this happens?

What if I change my university subject from law to philosophy?

- I will specialize in philosophy instead which I am going to find more interesting.
- I could find it harder to get regular employment after my degree.
- I will have to engage a different part of my brain and work differently.

What if this does not happen?

What if I do not change from law to philosophy?

- I will have to stick studying something I do not particularly like anymore.
- I will be always feeling that I should have changed.

What will happen if this happens?

What will happen if I change my subject from law to philosophy?

- I will have to catch up on study.
- I will be joining a new group.
- My parents may well be annoyed at my decision.
- All the hours spent studying law will now count as nothing.

What will not happen if this does not happen?

What will not happen if I do not change my subject from law to philosophy?

- I will not get to read the philosophers.

Dynamics of Discernment

- I will not be rid of subjects like land-law and commercial law which I hate.

These questions clarify the possible consequences of such decisions. The four questions show different angles to the decision/dilemma. So, we look at the same problem from four different perspectives, to help to make a conscious choice. We can ask:

1. What will I get from it?
2. Will everything stay the same? What are the advantages of not doing it?
3. What will not happen if this happens (the disadvantages of doing it)?
4. What will not happen if this does not happen (the disadvantages of not doing it)?

Example

To take another example: should someone stay in their existing job or move to another one?

1. What will happen if he changes jobs?
   - He will get the opportunity to learn more skills.
   - He will get to take on more responsibilities.
   - He will have to force himself to leave his comfort zone.
   - He will receive a large renumeration package.

2. What will happen if he does not change jobs?
   - He will keep his current way of life.
   - He will continue to worry about "what if".
   - He may blame or even hate himself for not taking this step.
   - He will remain on a lower salary scale.

3. What will not happen if he changes jobs?
   - He will not blame or hate himself for not taking this opportunity.
   - He must learn new skills.
   - He will not have any money worries.

4. What would not happen if he does not change jobs?
   - He will not have the stress connected to starting a new career.
   - He will not have the opportunity to grow his career.
   - He will not have to learn new skills needed for his new job.
   - He will not be able to pay off his mortgage earlier or afford a new car.

Of course, much will depend on one's education, imagination, experience, and qualifications. Also, it could be the case that you will want to get friends and family members involved in the decision-making process.

Assessment

Give a plus one (+1) to a positive answer and a minus one (-1) to a negative answer. Add up all the points, and if the sum is greater than zero, the recommendation is to change jobs (as in the case above). If the sum is less than zero, the recommendation would be not to change jobs. Decision-making is a skill that can be learnt. It takes time. It is important to give attention to the problem, and to understand the consequences. With Descartes, we think first before we leapfrog.

Thinking through the consequences of our decisions is also a theme of Massimo Pigliucci's Stoic algorithm of decision-making; the diagram from his book, *How to be a Stoic*, is reproduced below:

Words of the Wise

To recap on some of what we have been saying so far. We need to ask: do my fears dominate my decisions? How do I make decisions? Do I refer to the words of the wise? How we make decisions will shape our lives, so that the basis for our decision-making determines the decisions we make. Are my decisions reasonable? Are they motivated by love, goodness, and justice? Am I doing my duty or acting in conformity with my desires? When in doubt we should seek the advice of those who do not doubt. It is the discriminating mind (*buddhi*) rather than the discursive mind (*manas*) which discerns and decides. The intellect decides what is true. Our state of mind is important. The optimal state of mind with which to make big decisions is when the mind falls still—then it can see clearly and decide with certainty.

Dynamics of Discernment

We need to look to principles rather than to imagined consequences. Many decisions come from excessive attachments—you are certain about your wrong decision! The best decision is made when one is not invested in the outcome—when one can, in other words, detach.

Impediments to Decision-Making

These are to be avoided.

- *Desire*—disordered desire distorts decision-making.
- *Attachment*—being overly emotionally attached to the desired result.
- *Too much thinking*—excessive circular thinking derived from the monkey-mind. Analysis (thinking too long) is paralysis (will lead to doubt and procrastination). As Shakespeare's Hamlet put it "the native hue of resolution/ is sicklied o'er with the pale cast of thought"; "our natural boldness becomes weak with too much thinking. Actions that should be carried out at once get misdirected".
- *Postponement*—puting off until tomorrow those things you can do today. To everything there is a season.
- *Sentimentality*. Iris Murdoch speaks often of the perils of false sentimentality. Sentimentality softens and skewers things. In these cases, we do not face the facts but rather take refuge in fantasy.
- *Fear-factor* (or greed or doubt or excessive excitement)—these emotional factors damage decision-making.
- *Clairvoyancy*: we cannot foretell the future, so that to some extent, all decisions are made in the dark, in fear and trembling. Outcomes and consequences are the result of innumerable factors beyond our control.

Assets to Decision-Making

- *Stillness of the mind* ("be still and know that I am").
- *Good company* (this will bring out the best in you; the words of the wise can help with any decision).
- *Detachment* (letting go of the desire for a result or preferred outcome).

On Choosing and Deciding

- *Being your own best friend* (what advice would you give your best friend—then take this advice for yourself).
- *Conscience* (consult your Self—let yourself be led by the inner organ of meaning).
- *Socratize* (ask questions such as: is it good for me, my family, community, nation etc., always looking to the next level).
- *Unity* (search and try to discover the unity in every situation, rather than the division. Divisions are divisive. An Augustinian adage runs thus: "In essentials, unity; in non-essentials, liberty; in all things, love").
- *Philosophy* (the practical wisdom from the perennial tradition is a fount of knowledge).
- *Act under good authority* (true principles rather than personal preferences or possible predictions).
- *Carpe diem* (seize the day; obey the call of the hour, the imperative of the instant, the meaning of the moment).

If the action is good (the motivation pure), it will bear good fruit (beneficial results). "As ye sow, so shall ye reap" (the law of *karma*). Decisions may be based on any one of the following:

- Reason
- Love
- Virtue
- Duty
- Fear

The most important question you could ask is: What is the need here? Then, what is the motivation behind the task? Is it to satisfy my desire or the need of the moment?

So:

- Meet the need
- Act according to true principle
- Still the mind
- Open the heart

> "Shall I show you the sinews of a philosopher? What sinews are these?
> —A will undisappointed; evils avoided; powers daily exercised; careful resolution; unerring decisions."—Epictetus

> "I am not what happened to me. I am what I choose to become."—
> C. G. Jung

Buridan's Ass

There is a paradox in philosophy that goes back to Aristotle and on which a fourteenth-century philosopher, Jean Buridan, satirizes, in which a man (in Aristotle) or an ass (in later versions), is positioned between two necessities: food and drink (in Aristotle) and two bales of hay (in later versions). Buridan felt that pondering the outcomes could take so long one might starve to death—one could die before the choice was made. Jung mentions Buridan's ass three times in his writings.[20] The ass was not hungry, so he did not take the problem seriously. Carl Gustav Jung's point is this: when we externalize decisions, we look to an object (an outside authority) to make the choice. But good choices require us to look within. Leaving decisions to Fate or Destiny is abrogating, shirking responsibility, like Sartre's woman in the restaurant. Looking *within* is the key to making good choices. Free choice is a "subjective feeling of freedom" which is not totally free as one is will comes up against the limits of the world. There are inevitable conflicts (Hegel's master-slave dialectic). We often look outside for our authority (especially the hysteric, to put it in a Lacanian formulation, who hands her desire over to an Other—a master whom she looks for, but only in order to master). We thus externalize our decision-making. We may even look to an "act of God" in the form of a *fait accompli*. Jung did not favor either approach. Rather, he suggested we view situations as opportunities to hold the tension of opposites and wait for the resolution of the conflict in the emergence of the "transcendent function" (an operation not carried out by the ego but the Self). Such a process involves a waiting and a holding. We should recognize our "two-ness"—how we contain conflicting impulses and inclinations But a "third way" presents itself when we access the Self. Major life decisions are not *problems* to solve but *mysteries* to live with and through (to draw on philosopher Gabriel Marcel's distinction). Solutions

---

20. See Jung, *Collected Works*, 7 and 11.

are the purview of the ego. The Self provides, by contrast, a resolution in the appearance of the reconciling *third thing*, which opens up new perspectives and possibilities. Moreover, the man who has never really grown up (the *puer aeternus*) finds decisions difficult. He will need to integrate the *senex* (wise old man) who lies in his unconscious or else he will continue to live the provisional life and try to keep all his options permanently open. So, Jung's message is to awaken inward, to the Self. As he puts it: "Who looks outside, dreams. Who looks inside, awakes."[21]

The Four Villains of Decision-Making

"This OR that" (duality)? But what about deciding to do "this AND that"? (dialectics). The *four* villains of decision-making are:

1. Binary or narrow framing.
2. Confirmation bias—seeking out information that bolsters my belief.
3. Short-term greed rather than long-term gain.
4. Over-confident about our predictions.

That is a Wrap

To counter these tendencies, Chip and Dan Heath, authors of *Decisive,* propose a mnemonic model they call **WRAP**:

- **W**iden your options—expand your choices by shining a spotlight on them. Often our options are more plentiful than we think. Multitrack: consider more than one option simultaneously. Beware of sham options. When we develop only one choice, our ego is tied to it. Look outside yourself: to best practice, benchmarking etc. Look inside to your light (bright pots). Have a checklist, a playlist of new ideas that stimulate and suggest a way forward.
- **R**eality-test assumptions—obtain trustworthy information. Consider the opposite. This will counter the tendency of hunting for information that confirms our often self-serving assumptions. Disagreement and dissension counter confirmation bias. Find a good devil's advocate or

---

21. Jung, *C. G. Jung Letters*, 33.

Dynamics of Discernment

become one yourself. Zoom in and out. Rather than jumping in, test the waters first by dipping a toe in.

- **A**ttain distance before deciding—overcome short-term emotions. Do not let feelings engulf you. Practice the 10/10/10 rule. Consider future emotions not just present ones, asking "what will I do in ten days, ten months, ten years' time?" Contemplate the situation from an observer's perspective. Ask: "what would I tell my best friend to do in this situation?" Honor core priorities. Agonizing over decisions is often a sign of conflict. Decisions do not have to bind or break you.

- **P**repare to be wrong—be open to being refuted. The future is not a point we can predict—it is a range, a repertoire. We can carry out a premortem (example, "a year from now our decision failed. Why?"). We can anticipate possible obstacles so that they become opportunities. And for people who are coasting through life on autopilot, consider giving them deadlines.

I began this chapter considering choice, I would like to conclude it by exploring what Eastern philosophy has to say on the subject before, in the following chapter, looking at one particular system, which is extremely insightful and effective in relation to decision-making, and that is the Enneagram.

Two Alternatives: *Preya* and *Shreya*

At every moment we have a choice of *two* alternatives in what we:

- Think
- Say
- Do

They are:

- *Preya*: what is pleasant—it tickles the ego (*Ahamkāra*)
- *Shreya*: what is beneficial—it contributes to our peace of mind (*Shanti*).

Preya pleases us now, aiming for instant gratification ("if it feels good, do it"). *Shreya*, by contrast, may be unpleasant at the beginning, but it works to the good. (Sometimes, what is of lasting benefit is also pleasant, of course). For the most part, *Preya* and *Shreya* are in direct competition. Both promise

On Choosing and Deciding

satisfaction but *Shreya* shows us not the shadow but the substance of serenity. If our senses are taken in by *Preya* and sensory satisfactions, our reason directs us to *Shreya* and its substantial satisfactions. *Shreya* is the road that leads to wisdom. When you do not choose *Preya*, you are choosing *Shreya*. If you want to go East, just do not go West. This is the cardinal rule in making wise choices and decisions.

Prana and *Samskara*

We mentioned energy previously. *Prana* is undifferentiated energy. Just as the subtle body underlies the physical (gross) body, *prana* underlies all the expressions of physical energy: electromagnetic energy, gravitation, etc. The senses perceive when *prana* is present. But *prana* is also the energy of the mind. The force behind every desire is *prana*. *Prana* is power. When we love or reason or worry or choose or exercise our will to decide, we are drawing on *prana*. There is within us all a particular packet of *prana*. When the forces of the mind are controlled, *prana* is conserved (we are a psychosomatic unity). These forces are called *samskaras*. They are imprints, impressions. *Sam* means "intensely" and *kara* signifies "to do." Personality is a dynamic interplay of *samskaras*, of conditioned, mechanical habit. A *samskara* is a thought that is constantly repeated leading to words and actions that are repeated ten thousand times (Nietzsche's Eternal Recurrence). Personality is a process—the sum of our *samskaras*. We see life through our *samskaras* (personality projections). We are being shaped, sculpted by what we think, say, and do all the time. If desire is a river, *prana* flows along the channels created by *samskaras*. As it is put by the *Upanishads*: "You are what your deep, driving desire is. As your deep, driving desire is, so is your will. As your will is, so is your deed. As your deed is, so is your destiny".

Desire—Will—Deed—Destiny

Desire and will are close cousins; their surname is *prana*. There is will in every desire. The will is both friend and foe. Self-will is the power behind selfish desires. Selfish desire is suffering. The aim is to transform selfish desire into selfless service (self-transcendence), so that every negative *samskara* can be transformed and the personality reconfigured. We have a choice in what we think and therefore in what we say and do. Every choice (action) contains its consequences. Words and thoughts cause *karma*. From our thoughts flows everything: words, actions, desires, decisions, destiny. *Karma* is generated by our thinking and comes back to us through our conditioning. Really, according to the *Bhagavad Gita*, there are only *three* thoughts:

- Anger
- Fear
- Selfish desire

All these flow from self-will; from them come all *karma* and suffering too.

Two Selves: *Jiva* and *Purusha*

There are two selves in us, to put it metaphorically:

- *Jiva*—the individual ego
- *Purusha*—the indivisible *Ātman*

Jiva (individual self as sentient substance) is a bundle of sensations, which we call our personality—the flow/stream of consciousness. It is never the same at any two moments and yet we cling to it as if it were solid, but it is ever-shifting, constantly changing, fickle, fluid, and false. *Purusha* (person as spirit) is the real/true Self, another name for the *Ātman*. If *jiva* is the *persona* (mask), *purusha* is the face beneath all faces. These two are like shadow and substance. It is not that the shadow is unreal (we perceive it), it is just that it is not absolutely, only relatively real, just like our dreams. *Jiva* is all we see when the light of the Self is obstructed by self-will. This produces the grand illusion or *maya* (magic), occurring when we mistake the shadows on the wall of the cave (to draw on Plato's equivalent allegory) for reality itself. The Self, by contrast, is the detached, observer, simply watching, witnessing, and enjoying the show. The Self is the seed from which all things grow. In *samadhi* (meditative consciousness), all separateness fades, dissolves, and all division. *Maya* is the cosmic deception, delusion. In the land of unity, we see only the Self-same; in the land of duality, we see the Self as *maya*. *Maya* conceals, covers up, distorts but it also diverts our attention elsewhere, distracts us, telling us reality is out there in the spectacle of the sense-world. *Maya*'s magic wand is our desires. But without the radiance of the Self, none of the phenomenal world would exist. There may be billions of beings but there is only one sun, a single Self, shining on the sad and serene alike (on, what Viktor Frankl called the saints and the swine).

On Choosing and Deciding

"The decisive question for man is: Is he related to something infinite or not? That is the telling question of his life."—C. G. Jung

The seers and sages (*rishis*) have all realized the truth, which Aldous Huxley, following Leibnitz, calls the Perennial Philosophy because it appears in every age and epoch; its findings can be summarized in *three* statements:

1. There is in infinite, changeless reality beneath the world of change.
2. This same reality lies at the core of every human personality (human beings possess a double nature: a phenomenal ego and a Kierkegaardian "infinite inwardness").
3. The purpose of life is to discover this reality experientially.

The *Upanishads* contain the purest account of this timeless tradition, of the direct encounter (*shruti*) with the divine—the Absolute as both immanent and transcendent. *Brahman* is the Godhead—the Ground of being; *Ātman* is the divine core of the personality, the spark of the soul. *Dharma* is the law that expresses the unity of creation; *karma* is the web of cause and effect; *samsara* is the cycle of birth and death; and *moksha* is spiritual liberation, real freedom which is the goal of life. The Self or *Ātman* is the core of consciousness beyond change. *Ātman* is *Brahman*: the Self is each person is not different from the Godhead. Thus, *a-dvaita* meaning "not-two"—the One underlying the Many.

There are *three* states of ordinary consciousness: waking, dreaming, and dreamless (deep) sleep. Waking up (out of the dream of waking life) to the unitive state is the fourth, or *turiya*, where duality disappears. Going beyond *maya*—time, space, and causality is *samadhi*, whereby the state of *moksha* is attained (what Buddhists call *nirvana*).

Dharma is "that which supports" from within; it is the essence of a thing, the order of all things, its integrity. It signifies rightness, justice, harmony, purpose rather than chance. *Karma* is a deed done, an action. The law of *karma* states that every event is both a cause and an effect; every act(ion) has a consequence which produces other consequences and so on. There is an interconnectedness between mental and physical reality. Put simply, whatever you do will come back to you. A thought is like a seed—it sprouts a spreading tree. So, we begin by renouncing selfishness in thought, then word, then action. *Kama* is selfish desire. "Renounce and enjoy" is the injunction from the *Isha Upanishad*. This is doubly true for our choices and decisions.

Dynamics of Discernment

What do we want? The fourfold good (*chaturvarga*) consists of *dharma* (life in harmony with a higher power), *kama* (pleasure), *artha* (wealth), and *moksha* (liberation). We can satisfactorily achieve *kama*, *artha*, and *moksha* when *dharma* is our guide. "Individuation" is C. G. Jung's term for Self-realization. *Maya, karma,* and *dharma* have been called the school, the teacher, and the lesson. The call of *dharma* is the real intention of the soul (*psyche*). *Karma* emphasizes the freedom of choice. By the choices we make today, we retire the consequences of past actions and lay the foundation for a future of freedom. We are free to choose what actions to take in the present. Destiny does not preclude human freedom. Rather, it is the outcome of the actions we chose in the past whose effects create our present. Causality is the law of cause and effect. *Karma*, by contrast, implies we have the opportunity to modulate the impact of the past by our present choices, decisions, and actions. *Svadharma*—selfhood—is the summons to actualize our individual uniqueness. We engage with the creation with depth and detachment, and relinquish the fruit of all our actions. The transition from ego to Self enables us, in the words of the *Katha Upanishad*, "To pass from fearful fragmentation/To fearless fullness in the changeless whole."

2

Enneagram Discerning

THE ENNEAGRAM SYSTEM, WHICH may be described as a journey to the true Self, is arranged in the form of 3 X 3, with each enneatype being placed into one of *three* triads or centers of intelligence:

1. Instincts (body/gut/belly)
2. Feeling (heart)
3. Thinking (head)

The first type *go with their guts*; the second type *shoot straight from the heart*, feeling their way into situations; while the third type *think things through* ("it's all in your head"). These three centers or categories form a psychological Trinity. They are three basic orientations, ways in which individuals interact with others and the world. The gut people tend to be perfectionistic, protective, energetic, determined, action based. The feeling types are givers and doers, tragic romantics who are governed by their emotions, sensations, and moods. The thinking types tend to be observers, can be hedonists, relying on intellectual ideas, assessing information, analyzing behavior, and living in their imaginations.

The Enneagram maps out, in triadic form, adaptive patterns with great precision. It can help us to develop habits for wise decision-making in its framework of nine pilgrimages of personality, drawing as it does on philosophy, psychology, and spirituality. Each point in the enneagram system represents a particular *persona*. Every person contains aspects of all types, but they lead in life with one dominant enneatype which comprises a catalogue of habits, and which does not change. It is your egoic

Dynamics of Discernment

personality, your *adaptive* rather than *authentic* self. The dynamics of the Enneagram demonstrate how each type experiences stress (a coping mechanism) and security (a place of safety).

There are nine core desires: Ones want goodness but settle for order; Twos want unconditional love but settle for niceness; Threes want worth but settle for image; Fours want belonging but settle for longing; Fives want competency but settle for knowledge; Sixes want loyalty but settle for safety; Sevens want contentment but settle for excitement; Eights want protection but settle for control; and Nines want peace but settle for calm.

Types 8, 9 and 1 are belly or gut (instinctual) centered. Types 2, 3 and 4 are heart (feeling) centered, while types 5, 6 and 7 are head (thinking) centered. The question then becomes: Do we make decisions through our belly, head, or heart? The gut type makes decisions mainly according to intuition, as they respond almost immediately to their surroundings and to stimuli. The "feelers" are guided by their emotions, while the "head-cases" analyze, plan, think while making decisions.

Anger, shame, and fear are the triads' responses to anxiety. The gut-centered triad suffer from anger; the heart-centered triad suffer from shame; while the head-centered triad suffer from fear. All three emotions impede decision-making.

I have written about the nine types in *The Nine Faces of Fear*, so here I will concentrate on them solely in relation to decision-making. But first, below is a list of the nine types.

1. The Reformer
2. The Helper
3. The Achiever
4. The Individualist
5. The Investigator
6. The Loyalist
7. The Enthusiast
8. The Challenger
9. The Peacemaker

- Ones want to do what is right
- Twos are worried about what others think

- Threes ask what the most efficient choice is
- Fours say to themselves "I"ll really have to ponder on this"
- Fives need all the facts before they decide
- Sixes see that the worst thing to do is make no decision at all
- Sevens enquire "what are all my options here?"
- Eights simply act from gut
- Nines wonder whether they have to decide right now

We make small and big decisions daily and the cycle time for so doing has never been faster. The Enneagram, as an application, can greatly help us to understand our decision-making dynamics and style, as well as that of others. It can guide us in making decisions with head, heart, and gut, thus giving full voice to the thinker, the feeler, and the doer dwelling inside all of us.

The Nine Questions of Discernment

Discernment is a gift, a process, is complex and holistic, and requires self-knowledge, courage, and humility. According to Drew Moser in his book, *The Enneagram of Discernment*, when facing a decision, we should consider the following:

- Who am I? (Identity)
- Why am I here? (Purpose)
- Where am I going? (Direction)

- What am I doing? (Gut center)
- What am I feeling? (Heart center)
- What am I thinking? (Head center)

- What am I remembering? (Past)
- What am I experiencing? (Present)
- What am I anticipating? (Future)

Dynamics of Discernment

Ego vs Self

We tend to reply too much on the false self. Here, my identity subsists in my ego-personality, so that we can distinguish *three* lies at the heart of personal identity:

- I am what I have.
- I am what I do.
- I am what others say about me.

The Empty Ps of this false self are: pleasure, praise, power, prestige, position, popularity, people, productivity, possessions. The false/adapted self is the result of an over-identification with our *ego* rather than our *essence*. The ego conspires in our division and diminishment. By contrast, the Self is spacious, integral wholeness and awareness, which leads to *shalom* or flourishing—what the ancient Greek philosophers called *eudaimonia*. Discernment requires we enquire:

- What am I doing?
- What am I feeling?
- What am I thinking?

The Three Centers and Stances

The *three* centers of knowing (triadic self) are body (gut), mind, and heart. Each is a hub of knowing, and meaning-making—a thinking intelligence, a feeling intelligence, and a doing intelligence: thoughts, feelings, actions. We have a gut intelligence ("GQ")—here the gut leads in decision-making; a heart intelligence ("EQ")—here emotions dominate in decision-making; and a head intelligence ("IQ"), where thoughts predominate in decision-making.

The *three* stances are the Aggressive Stance (types Three, Seven, and Eight), the Dependent Stance (types One, Two, and Six), and the Withdrawn Stance (types Four, Five, and Nine). The first group of the triad "move against" others. They *think* and *do* their way through life, misusing or distorting *feeling*. The second group "move forward"—they act alongside others. They *do* and *feel* their way through life, often neglecting *thinking*. The third group "draw back." They think and feel their way through life at the expense of right *action*. Discernment and decision-making demand that we deploy our full range of thinking (mind), feeling (heart), and doing (body). What are my head-brain, heart-brain and gut-brain telling me?

- How do my thoughts make wise decisions?
- How do my feelings make wise decisions?
- How do my actions make wise decisions?

Let us delve a bit more deeply into the various types and the respective decision-making processes involved.

Ones

Ones are perfectionistic. They trust their instinct; they tend to decide quickly. They use their mind to make sense of their reactions. Their anger is their greatest hindrance. For Ones, objectivity is king. They think about what they should do rather than what they subjectively want. They try to do the "right" thing. They need to consider a variety of alternative choices. They should try to turn their decision-making into more of an art form and use a well-paced action to get good results. Their moral compass can help others make ethically informed decisions. Unhealthy (unredeemed) Ones can be rigid and demand their own way when it comes to making decisions. They feel that theirs is the moral high ground. They are rational, reasonable, competent, reliable, intuitive in decision-making, hard-working, self-controlled, productive, and notoriously ethical. They navigate decision-making with a strong inner moral compass and struggle to make decisions congruent with their values and vision. They can be rigid, critical, domineering, and controlling. They are quite smart but can misuse their thinking intelligence. Their integrity and intuition are significant resources in decision-making. They can become fixated by "shoulds" and "oughts"; they need to be more playful when it comes to decision-making. Ones are persuaded by the greater good—the team or company or the work itself. The One's best friend is the Law; they can be judgmental. Once Ones make decisions, they obsess about them afterwards. But Ones can be great facilitators of consensus. Ones get things done regardless of the consequences.

Dynamics of Discernment

Twos

Twos want love. They are sensitive as well as anxious about life and this stress manifests itself as shame. Twos rely on their feeling-sense and effect on others whom they enlist to follow their decisions. They may have difficulty making decisions that could generate resistance and negatively impact others as they are always enquiring about the needs of others. Interpersonal issues and emotional factors are usually at play when a Two decides. Twos should try and make decisions without their personal feelings getting in the way and find the balance between facts and feelings. Healthy Twos tend to be altruistic, empathic, and compassionate when it comes to making a decision. They will look to their values/ethics and consider the impact on others. Unhealthy Twos may steamroll over the needs of others and make decisions that are in their "best" interest, only to end up resenting them later on. Their flattery can feed their subtle pride. They want to be needed. In decision-making they show relational energy and can connect well with a group. Theirs is a positive presence which can cognitively reframe conflict—a contagious sweetness. If Sevens are enthusiasts who recruit, Twos are enthusiasts who impress. They are assertively nice, adaptable, and excellent listeners, generous (they can sacrifice themselves selflessly) and strategically helpful. Their relationships animate their decision-making. They never want to disappoint. They fear both rejection and inferiority. They tend to misuse their thinking intelligence—it can become unproductive. They can become scattered and disorganized. They can cede their cognition to others, and bring past experiences into the present. They can read the room well. Twos like to be indispensable—they like to know they are having an impact. Logical argumentation and ethical standards of procedures do not convince them. Twos can bend rules if peoples" feelings are at stake. Twos shoot from the hip, like Sevens; they are similarly straight talkers. They listen to themselves and rely on hunches, on intuitions, and impressions rather than reasoning. Twos are helpers, demanding to be appreciated.

Threes

Threes are achievers who want to be worthy. They image-craft to impress. They present as polished, determined, accomplished, goal oriented. They can feel anxious about life, which exhibits itself as shame. They rapidly consider options, weighing up pros and cons of each, before quickly moving on to action-plans. Their decisions may be efficient or expedient but not necessarily effective. They need to be cognizant of this. Threes are decisive and self-reliant and make decisions that lead to their (and others") success, weighing up the pros and cons with haste. They have little patience for procrastination and dawdling. They are goal-setters but also dreamers and can energize and inspire others, but they can also make decisions in a spirit of competitiveness and self-interest and manipulate others to reach what they perceive as a higher rung on the ladder of success. Threes tend to perceive decisions in their heart center. They quickly engage in either productivity or distraction, especially in the face of perceived failure, and feel motivated and excited about the result of a decision. They are often in a state of productive procrastination; they are both assertive and pragmatic in groups. They are driven to excel and seem equipped with limitless energy. They are competitive and savvy, putting themselves in a position to succeed. They take calculated risks, set goals and network well. Unhealthy Threes can be vain, vindictive, and narcissistic. They like information and tend to fixate on what is next. They need to engage their heart center more. They live a mile wide but an inch deep. This is a danger. They over-rely on a thinking and doing intelligence. They will repress their feelings to get the job done. They are confident in decision-making—theirs is a polished impulsivity. They can become workaholics who struggle with failure. Threes are linear in their decision-making; they make a beeline for their goals. They like to tell and sell. That is their decision-making style. They are salesmen who like to be sold. Fours focus on results, responding best to the bottom line, to cost benefits. Threes keep decisions simple—they like clear cut comparisons. They rush to closure. They are producers, who work hard to succeed.

Fours

Fours are individualists who want to belong. Their stress manifests as deficiency. They shun the ordinary, the mundane. They tend to isolate and retreat into their emotions—they feel intensely and are nostalgic for the past. Fours experience themselves as misunderstood and self-scrutinize. They can be emotionally reactive, dramatic even. But they are creative, aesthetic, discerning, imaginative. They tend to introject others. They make well-considered, value-based decisions which may make them appear slow to decide as they take their time and will not be rushed, particularly if they feel compromised. They stay true to their values, guided by their guts as to what is right and wrong. They need to be encouraged to deploy logic as well as intuition, facts as much as feelings in their decision-making deliberations. They can get stuck in indecision, especially if trying to please or placate someone. They should guard against making sweeping decisions particularly those wrapped up in feelings. They are prone to procrastination. Fours make decisions by comparisons. They do not care too much about objectivity. Their decision-making reflects their personal, emotional truth and perception. Their decisions emanate from feeling-based intuitions. Fours, despite appearances to the contrary, are introverts who look to their internal processes for decision-making. They are creative connoisseurs with a penchant for the dramatic.

Fives

Fives are investigators who want competency. They fear being useless and empty; this fear which they carry impedes their decision-making. They are curious about the workings of things and have an allergy to superficial small-talk and high-energy social engagement. They are logical and reason their way through decisions with their head-center, assessing all the relevant facts, analyzing, and organizing. They are conscientious. "Facts first" is their motto. They need abundant information (always wanting more) which may not be possible to attain, in order to feel comfortable with any given decision. They should know that decisions can be made faster when heart, gut, and head are integrated. They rush decisions even though (or because) they struggle with analysis-paralysis. Healthy Fives do not dig through every available piece of information and remain open-minded, careful, insightful, even if not as decisive as Threes or Eights, guided by intuition. Unhealthy Fives find it hard to decide, stuck in preparedness mode, mulling things over endlessly, struggling to discern what is relevant and drowning in irrelevant information. In these cases, their decisions are often the fruit of frustration. They value privacy and space and are non-conformists. Their vice is avarice—they hold onto things, finding it hard to relinquish. They are possessive over their thoughts and tend to get fixated on past perspectives. They are rational rather than relational and these skills make them effective in decision-making. Fives are sages who crave data and theories but forget the human element. They are analytic, wanting to know what makes things tick. Fives look for formulas. They are cool and detached, so emotionally charged decisions will not rattle them. Their decisions are logical, elegant, unfettered by sentiment. They make ratiocinative, precise decisions: "just the facts please." They are controlled and stand apart and their decision-making reflects this stance. Fives love decision-trees—indeed, any analytical tool, preferably complicated with several choice points. When making decisions, they do not like being put under pressure or given deadlines or demands. They need information, facts, evidence, logic. Then they need to be let at it. "Show me the numbers" is their catch-cry. Their decisions can seem like edicts—*faits accompli*, because Fives rarely share their personal process. In this sense, they can come across as intimidating as Eights.

Sixes

Sixes are loyalists who want to be supported. They fear being in an unfaithful environment. They lack fundamental trust in others. They are suspicious, cautious, on-guard. They think through the impact of all possible decisions including situations or scenarios where obstacles might arise. Because of this, they become anxious—even paralyzed—when making decisions or they make impulsive ones as they create so many options for themselves, generate so many possibilities. They are looking for security, certainty, are risk adverse. They need to trust themselves, more perhaps by asking what they would advise someone else to do in a similar situation. Healthy Sixes are trustworthy, thoughtful, skilled and make sacrifices. Unhealthy Sixes are trapped in indecision and agonize over every petty detail, often choosing the "safest" course of action. Sixes are intuitive, practical, sensible, worry-warts, indeed, the pessimists of the Enneagram. They are dutiful, responsible, collaborative, steadfast team-players. They see through false pretenses and hidden agendas. Their primary defense is projection, which is a way of dispensing with their misanthropic mistrust. They tend to split, separating people into good and bad. Their feelings and doings can take over and they can become quite paranoid. Sixes struggle with making decisions, becoming visibly anxious. They obsess about the future. They can feel fatigued by their present and overwhelmed. Sixes like to know the dangers lurking in decisions—the potential problems. If you do not present the Six with the negatives, he will think you have not done your homework. Expose your self-interest, as Sixes do not find altruism completely credible. Unlike Nines, Sixes have no problem deciding—they make decisions rapidly, but then they stew over them. They are most at home in their heads. They decide by analysis. If Threes decide by way of comparisons, Sixes decide by way of historical analogy—they ruminate over past events, customs, and traditions, looking for precedent. Do not be in a hurry if you need a decision from a Six—they need "to think about it." Share your facts and arguments with them. Sixes want to know everyone else's position before assuming their own on any subject, which makes spontaneous, on-the-spot decisions pretty difficult. Sixes are trouble-shooters who can get quite paranoid.

Sevens

Sevens are enthusiasts who want contentment. They fear being deprived and in pain. Their tendency to hyper-plan can cause them to overlook the present. They are idealistic, charmingly assertive, energetic, optimistic and can reframe pretty much any negative and turn it into a positive. Sevens seem to have magical qualities—they charm and disarm. They are curious, imaginative, spontaneous, and have an uncanny ability to diffuse tension through humor. They scheme, plan, plot, and recruit. They are ever the tourist, rarely the resident. They perceive, indeed "entertain," multiple options for possible decisions as well as a variety of pathways for execution. They may make decisions too hastily, based on a good idea, but without the necessary deliberation. They need to make sure that they have all the data at their disposal, and not just the highlights or summary. They worry about making the wrong decision and missing out as a result. They tend to make practical decisions by blending their enthusiasm, excitement, and enjoyment. They get the best out of a situation. They see if their decisions match their values. Unhealthy Sevens chase distractions with scant regard for outcomes. They make impulsive choices and become overly anxious. They tend to choose the most fun option and ignore hard or painful decisions altogether or they focus on something else which they would prefer to be doing. They resent being rushed and may show their impatience, snapping at others. Their glass-half-full approach to life can overcompensate and cloud their judgement. They can find it hard to see things through to completion, and struggle to be fully present. They often abandon projects. For Sevens, freedom reigns supreme. They are fully committed to not being fully committed. Their rebelliousness permits them to indulge in an epicurean excess of life. Their eye is always on the future. Sevens seek levity, fun, and adventure. They get bored easily. They need to let their heart catch up with their head (and body). Their buoyant positivity can lighten the mood of any room but their fixation on excitement can impede their ability to discern with depth. They are usually engaged with multiple things all at once, and when on vacation they are planning their next vacation. They are joyful jugglers who thrive on variety. But less is sometimes better and they can become cocooned in a cage of unrealistic and disappointed expectation. Their catch-cry: "what's next? I cant wait." Sevens struggle with patience, seeking quick fixes and hits of excitement. They want to be enthralled. Closure frightens Sevens because when possibilities come to an end, so does the adventure. Their decisions take places against a kaleidoscopic and ever-changing background of people and ideas. Sevens are excellent brainstormers. They are imaginative visionaries who inspire and lead.

Eights

Eights have no trouble making decisions. They make instantaneous, gut-based decisions that include the big picture, but they may not consult with others and this can leave them behind or not on board with the action. They like being in charge and taking control, disliking dilly-dallying decision-makers. They should question their assumptions more and slow down the decision-making process. They can dictate, wanting to make decisions which bring them close to realizing their goals. They are assertive, protective. Unhealthy Eights fear others are turning against them or chipping away at their freedom. So, they tend to rush decisions in order to re-assert themselves and wreak revenge on others. Eights are challengers who believe that the best defense is offense. They are assertive, black and white, declarative, forceful, direct, intense. They have a compulsion to conquer. Feelings can signal weakness to the Eight, so they need to cultivate their feeling-intelligence more when making decisions. Eights are centrally concerned with justice and fair play so all their decisions will reflect their core interest. Appeal to their desire to settle scores and their sense of right and wrong. Eights like to test themselves. They do not have the patience to explore unconscious dynamics. They like people to move toward them and they go by their gut. Haste makes waste. Some Eights act as dictators and will not take cognizance of your opinion while others will pay lip-service to participatory democracy. They will continue to make decisions behind closed doors. They are not swayed by the preponderance of other peoples' opinions or decisions. Eights are top dogs who exercise leadership but may end up as vengeful bullies.

Dynamics of Discernment

Nines

Nines are peacemakers but under stress become passive-aggressive. They integrate different viewpoints, using a 360-degree perspective, one which co-opts others through consensus. They can feel extremely pressurized when asked to make unilateral or controversial decisions. They are harmonious mediators, seeing many sides to a situation. They need to consult with their gut and listen carefully. They often struggle with indecision because they are unsure how it will affect others. They do not shove their feelings down the necks of others. They assert themselves considerately and compassionately. Unhealthy Nines simply refuse to make any decisions, opting out entirely of the decision-making process, leaving it to others to pick up the pieces. They retreat from the world, withdraw into themselves, rejecting all forms of external pressure. The danger is that they will make decisions that please or silent others, disregarding their own needs in the process. They are conciliatory, deferential, quietly pragmatic, and portray a positive outlook. They tend to be lazy and merge with the desire of others. They are supportive, attentive, and effective consensus builders when it comes to decision-making. Thy are stable and will not be rushed or hurried when making a decision. Nines are relaxed, methodical, and pleasant-natured, optimistic but they find it difficult to get going. They are accommodating and compliant but struggle with discernment, abdicate authority and are quite stubborn. They can shut themselves off from listening. They are especially prone to self-narcotization. They over-rely on thinking and feeling and are lethargic when it comes to actually doing anything. They go to sleep on the essential issues. Their daydreams disengage them from deciding. Nines are ruminators who go back and forth and chew the cud before committing to any decision. They are hard to pin down. Their tactic is to avoid decisions by requesting more information, or by counselling prudence or restraint. By insisting that everyone is heard, they postpone decision-making. Nines need their decisions to be corroborated. Decisions are difficult for the Nine because it involves laying claim to something. They get stressed when bombarded by decisions and choices. Nines accommodate nicely and adjust. They want everyone to work in a conflict-free zone. In so doing, they tend to forget their own goals along the way.

Sankofa

"Sankofa" is a West African concept which captures the essence of discernment and the Enneagram journey, we have been exploring, from ego to Self. *Sankofa* is a mythical bird with its body forward and head turned backward. Roughly translated as "go back and get it," it is a reminder that we must remember to fetch what is in danger of being left behind.

- *SAN* (return): to our original identity as Self (*imago Dei*).
- *KO* (go): forward with flourishing, meaning and purpose, fathoming our depth and direction.
- *FA* (look): to the present moment and engage with it fully in terms of our head, heart, and gut (the cultivation of wisdom).

3

Creativity

Psyche-Evoking

THE ANCIENT PHILOSOPHICAL TERM for soul is *psyche* (our word "psychology" is a *logos* of the *psyche*). *Psyche* is the place of depth and height, as well as the principle of direction (it shows the movement of the life). Depth refers to the magnitude of being. For Ira Progoff (1921–1998), the American psychologist, one-time student of C. G. Jung, and founder of the intensive journal method, psychology begins as an unconscious search for meaning. It was Plato, however, who first postulated the necessity for a *care of the soul* and saw man as a being in search of meaning.

Each person's life is an artwork; the nature of the *opus* unfolds in *psyche* as life proceeds. By paying attention to *psyche*, our awareness enlarges. Messages are given to us in the twilight range of experience, according to Progoff, in symbolic forms. There is a process going on within us of symbolic unfoldment. Such inner images (the imagery of the *psyche*) are intimations in our journey to wholeness (providing clues of what is to come in the life of the person).[1]

"The image carries the energy of hope."—Ira Progoff

The *psyche* is always in flow; it is a movement of many kinds of images by which we may discover the meaning of our personal existence. However,

---

1. For this and much of what follows, ee especially Progoff, *At a Journal Workshop* and *The Symbolic and the Real*.

Creativity

our personal life takes place against the backdrop of universal/transpersonal archetypes. Our life-task is to align our outer work with the inner *opus*. The image of our individuality—what Progoff calls the "dynatype"—sets the requirements of our individual life. For Jung and Progoff, dreams and myths are the primary premium for intuitive insights into the ultimate nature of existence. The process of symbolic unveiling is the essence of creative growth. In therapy, Progoff will have us draw on (in order to gain access to) the sources of the stream rather than chip endlessly away at the boulder. Psychotherapeutic work is best carried out, he contends, not by *analyzing* the patient but by *evoking* their depths. To this end, he developed the technique of "twilight imaging," thus extending the work of Jung and Otto Rank.

A symbol appears as a spontaneous image from the depth of the personality and acts as a vehicle by which the person's potential can be carried forward. To be sure, the potential lies already dormant in the seed-depths of the individual. The work is to draw it forth. Progoff gives the example of Socrates before the court in Athens. His two sources were an *outward* (the gods of the Greek pantheon) and *inward* one (the oracle within himself, what Socrates himself called "the divine faculty"). The aim is always the same: to awaken from unawareness. Where Socrates's way was a goading (he was described as a gadfly), the corresponding psychological way is "psyche-evoking." The *psyche* (as metaphor) denotes the "place" of integrative wholeness, of luminous consciousness. We need to move from asking the Freudian question, "what is the *psyche* hiding?" to "what is it trying to unfold?": from pathology to potentiality. The organic *psyche* (Progoff's term) or the objective *psyche* (Jung's term) is the directive principle guiding growth; it discloses itself in the pattern of events that comprise a person's biography, in his work in the world, his social relations (outwardly) and inwardly as dreams, images, intuitions etc. To repeat: inner images reveal a pattern of meaning and a direction of development.

> "The psyche is a mirror of the patterns of meaning that give form to the infinite."—Ira Progoff

Progoff would ask the patient to close his eyes, relax and permit himself to observe and describe the flow of imagery that moves upon the screen of his mind's eye. This flow is a product of the image-making faculty of the *psyche*—it is kaleidoscopic rather than telescopic. What is taking place in the organ depths of the psyche with its protoplasmic images is *psychic* reality.

Dynamics of Discernment

The expression (rather than repression) of such symbolic enactment is creative through and through; it makes possible vital new experiences of meaning. When life is experienced symbolically as part of the spiritual growth of the person, symptoms disappear because they are given no attention; they thus find themselves out of place. The key is simply to describe (phenomenologically) the symbolic material without analyzing or interpreting it. The best progress is made when the attention shifts away from the symptom (what Viktor Frankl calls "dereflection") to the depth level of the *psyche* (its *logos*). In this way of working, we reach toward the ideal of Socrates, for the individual gets a chance to experience his existence from an inward point of view and what is there disclosed is nothing other than the Self as spiritual reality. Progoff thus places the person in dialogue with the unfoldment of his life, so that a dialectical relationship is established with external events and interior experiences. The hope is that by accessing the powerful tool of imagination, we become "artists-in-life".

In Greek mythology, Psyche is a mortal woman who becomes the wife of Eros and thus divine. In psychology, *psyche* refers to the totality of the personality—both conscious and unconscious dimensions. Psyche is the goddess of the soul and the wife of Eros (Roman Cupid), god of love. So, soul (*psyche*) and love (*eros*) are inextricably linked in mythology. Once a mortal princess, her beauty earned her the ire of Aphrodite (Roman Venus) when the girl began to get worshipped rather than the goddess. Aphrodite commanded Eros to make Psyche fall in love with the most hideous man—himself—this loathsome little seducer, but when Eros saw Psyche, he fell in love with her. He decided not to carry out his mother's commandment—that Psyche was to be in love with the worst possible specimen of humanity—possessed by base and consuming erotic passion. Many men made pilgrimages to Psyche to see her beauty, but none sought her hand in marriage. Psyche's father sought advice from the Delphic oracle and was told she would be set on a lofty mountain rock and wed a snakelike monster. Psyche goes to the top of the mountain and steps off to be rescued and is taken to a golden palace. Eros makes love to her at night when she cannot see him and becomes invisible during the day. Soon, Psyche becomes pregnant. Despite all the wealth, Psyche is lonely and begs her husband to let her sisters visit her despite his warning that they would bring about her downfall. The sisters visit her and become jealous on seeing her wealth and thinking that her husband is a god. They eat, chat and Psyche gives them riches to carry off. They return

Creativity

home and begin to moan about her and decide they would punish her for her arrogance. They go to visit her once more. In the meantime, Eros tells her that if she discloses information about her husband the child will be mortal but a deity if the secret is kept. Psyche is then told by some criminals that once her child is born, she/he will be eaten by her husband who is really a serpent. She decides to get a dagger to kill him. But she pricks herself on one of Eros's arrows and falls deeply in love with her husband. As she kisses him, she accidentally drops oil from her lamp and burns his shoulder. He wakes up and sees his wife holding a knife and takes fright. Eros departs to get healed. Psyche tells her sisters that Eros now wants them, so they both jump off the mountain tops and kill themselves. Psyche searches for her husband and comes upon a temple belonging to Demeter, then one belonging to Hera. They tell her that Aphrodite is looking for her. Aphrodite goes to Hermes and says no man or god should shelter her. Aphrodite finds her and sets awful tasks for her to do. Her final chore is to go down to Hades. Lastly, Psyche and Eros have a daughter—Hedone.

We are all engaged in various works, in specific projects or outer activity that draws from an inner source (the *psyche* or "soul"). It may take external form, but the meaning and direction come from the person. All works begin in the depths of the human being, as a hint or a hunch, forming the desire to create. The self unfolds in the work, just as a tree begins from a seed. The work (artwork) and the person (artist) stand in a mutually creative relation to one another. So, we distinguish (but only in order to unite) the inward movement of energy that activates the image within the person on which the work will be based, which sets the possibility and the goal, and the outward movement which is the focused activity by which the seed of possibility that is present in the work is brought forth to fruition. Let us embark on "doing the work" through journaling.

Steppingstones

Exercise: List the varied works (deeds done) that have been meaningful to you in the course of your life—what Progoff calls "steppingstones." Look back over this period and ask yourself: "what were the most meaningful activities for you," which had "inner importance." Try to identify these artworks/goals that had an inner meaning for you. What are the ones that now awaken within you twinges of excitement, tingles, mobilizing the energy of emotion? Recall them and make a list.

Dynamics of Discernment

_____

_____

_____

_____

_____

_____

_____

_____

You will find that this imaginative exercise often leads to new insights, the seed of future work and decisions. Let these meaningful works come to you when sitting in stillness. Now, reread your list, amplifying it with brief comments, with a word or a phrase, or an emotion or a thought or a memory. Direct your attention to these artworks. List the steppingstones—the process and path by which you arrived there. When did it begin? What led to this decision, this choice? What gave rise to the idea or inspiration that brought your work (deed) into being? What were the events that enabled it to continue? What difficulties did it encounter? What feelings have you about it? What is the situation now? Just sit in stillness, eyes closed, allowing your breathing to become slower, relaxing your body, letting your concerns drop away and dissolve, turning your attention to the life of the work, recording its beginnings, its phases of development, direction, and difficulties, perceiving the continuity of its life-history. Let images come to you unguided; simply observe these symbolic forms—these twilight images that are psyche-evoking. Speak to the work as it speaks with you. See the steppingstones ("stations of the soul"—the significant points of movement along the road of your life) you made to get to this point. Record the feelings you had while this inner dialogue took place. These steppingstones are the *markings* of a life history.

Creativity

Intersections: Roads Taken and Not Taken

Exercise: This one is based on an image of the road, passing through many environments, sometimes taking detours, shifting direction, avoiding obstacles. Very often we had to make our decisions in the midst of the pressure of events, when travelling at full speed. We pause now to consider our life in retrospect, recognizing the choices that we made at those intersections. We discern that there are *two* roads in our life: the roads we actually travelled and the roads we did not take. What we found on the road we travelled is known to us; it comprises and contains the content of our life as lived. The other untaken roads are unknown to us. They remain as possibilities. List all the Intersections, all the Roads Taken and Not Taken, that you can think of in your life as a whole. The list of Steppingstones can remind you of Intersections at various points of your life.

Dynamics of Discernment

_____

_____

_____

_____

Sometimes at a crossroads a difficult decision has to be made. Sit in quiet, yes closed and look inward, placing yourself on the road of your life. See the Intersections, the alternative roads. Go down one of the roads to see where it leads and observe what you find along the way. Then you can come back to the intersection and go up the other road. When you have seen what is on both roads, you will be able to make your decision. See if you can do this. The imagery will give you guidance, a sense of inner knowing, drawing up energy from the organ depths of your *psyche*, through symbolic forms which become self-disclosing.

These imaginative exercises give perspective, depth, direction, providing a compass to the true north—the special meaning of your unique life. We do not *diagnose* but enable a life to *disclose* meaning through inward attention. It is a depth-psychological process of self-enquiry, drawing one's personal life into focus, a procedure which leads to a progressive deepening. As Jung and Frankl recognized—there is no lasting healing without an experience of meaning at the depth of one's being.

Models of Creativity

Creativity is a process whereby something new is formed, something original is produced. It could be an idea, an invention, a theory, a solution. Here, we can distinguish Four Ps.

- Process—the thought mechanisms and techniques for creative thinking.
- Product—measuring the product by psychometrics.
- Person—the focus here is on the person's ideation.
- Place—looks at the circumstances in which creativity flows and flourishes.

Creativity

The word "creativity" comes from the Latin "*creo*" meaning "to create" or "to make." (It appears in English in the fourteenth century with Chaucer). In Plato and Aristotle, the word is *mimesis* or imitation, which is not really creativity proper. As Plato puts it in the *Republic*: "Will we say of a painter that he makes something? Certainly not, he merely imitates." It was not until the Enlightenment that the notion of imagination becomes apparent. A five-stage model was proposed by psychologist Graham Wallas in the twentieth century, to explain creative insights and illuminations.[2]

- *Preparation*—the preparatory work on a problem that focuses the mind on the problem. The conscious mind surveys, works, flounders, exhausts itself.
- *Incubation*—where the problem is internalized in the unconscious and nothing external appears to be happening. It lingers latently.
- *Intimation*—the creative person gets a "feeling" that a solution is imminent.
- *Illumination* (or insight)—where the creative idea bursts forth from its preconscious processing into conscious awareness. It comes as a flash, suddenly.
- *Verification*—when the idea is consciously consolidated, elaborated, presented to the public and then applied (the aftermath).

James Kaufman introduced a Four C model of creativity:[3]

- Mini-c: transformative learning involving personally meaningful, interpretation of experiences, actions, and insights
- Little-c: everyday problem-solving and creative expression
- Pro-c: exhibited by people who are professionally or vocationally creative
- Big-C: creativity considered great in a given field

Creative people are capable of divergent thinking (mediated by the frontal lobe). *Three* components of creativity are needed:

- Expertise (technical, procedural, and intellectual knowledge)

---

2. Wallas, *Art of Thought*. Originally a four-stage model, Wallas's model eventually incorporated "Intimation," adding a fifth stage.
3. Kaufman and Beghetto, "Beyond Big and Little."

- Creative thinking skills
- Motivation (especially intrinsic)

Extrinsic motivation consists of external factors such as money or threats; intrinsic motivation comprises satisfaction, enjoyment, purpose, and meaning. To encourage motivation, we can engage with *six* practices:

- *Challenge*—matching people with the right assignments.
- *Freedom*—giving people autonomy to pursue goals.
- *Resources*—time, space, and money.
- *Group support*—mentors, work buddies, teams.
- *Supervisory encouragement*—recognitions, praise.
- *Organizational support*—collaboration, information-sharing.

Creativity has been identified as one of the 4 Cs of twenty-first century living, indeed, identified as the most important skill:

- Critical thinking
- Communication
- Collaboration
- Creativity

Day-Dreaming

In his famous article from 1908, "Creative Writers and Day-Dreaming," Sigmund Freud begins by asking: "From what sources that strange being, the creative writer, draws his material, and how he manages to make such an impression on us?"[4] His answer: *the origins of creativity lies in childhood.* The child's best-loved and most intense occupation is play or games. Freud asserts: "every child at play behaves like a creative writer" in that he creates a world of his own. He treats play very seriously. The opposite of play is not what is serious but what is real. "The creative writer does the same as the child at play."[5] Creativity is the play of phantasy. For the Freudian, the function of creativity is sublimation and compensation; for the Aristotelian it serves as a *catharsis*, a purgation of the passions, especially of pity and

1. Freud, "Creative Writers," 436.
5. Freud, "Creative Writers," 437.

Creativity

fear. When a child grows up, he ceases to play; they surrender this yield of pleasure. Actually, Freud contends, we never give up anything, only exchange one thing for another. What appears as a renunciation is really the formation of a substitute or surrogate. Instead of playing, he now fantasizes; he builds up castles in the air and creates daydreams. A child's play is determined by wishes (example, the wish to be grown up). For Freud, a happy person never fantasizes, only an unhappy one. The motive force of fantasies are unsatisfied wishes. Every fantasy (or with a "ph" to denote unconscious phantasies) is the fulfilment of a wish (just like a dream), a correction of unsatisfying reality. And wishes can be either a) ambitious or b) erotic. In women, ambition is absorbed by eroticism, in men by egoism. Daydreams hark back to a memory of an earlier experience (an infantile one) to which this wish was fulfilled, only now it creates a situation relating to the future which represents a fulfilment of the wish. The past, present, and future are strung together on the thread of the wish that runs through them. If phantasies become over-powerful, the conditions are laid for an onset of neurosis or psychosis. Our night-dreams are nothing other than phantasies. Myths and legends are, according to Freud, the distorted vestiges of the wishful phantasies of whole nations, "the secular dreams of youthful humanity." A writer, so, presents us with his personal daydreams and we experience a great pleasure ("the aesthetic yield of pleasure"): i.e., the pleasure-principle (by contrast to the reality-principle). Our enjoyment of an imaginative world proceeds from a liberation of tensions in our mind. The writer enables us to enjoy our own daydreams without reproach.

Playing

Subsequent analysts such as Donald Winnicott and Viktor Frankl interpreted creativity in a much more benign light. In *Playing and Reality*, Winnicott puts forward the notion of a "transitional object" which oscillates between the inner and outer worlds. For Winnicott, culture and creativity develop from a *transitional space*. He emphasizes the primacy of play in life. His own research draws on his study of mothers and infants. An example of a transitional object would be a piece of cloth or a teddy-bear. It is the first "not-me" phenomenon, an intermediate area where are inner and outer worlds are interrelated. These cloths or blankets act as defenses against anxiety. Winnicott then broadens the discussion out to artistic creativity. Like Freud, he relates a child's play to an adult's creativity.

Dynamics of Discernment

The two areas overlap and interweave. Therapy encourages people to play. Playing occurs in a potential space of meaning (in the child between it and mother). Playing facilitates health; it is a form of communication. After playing, the next stage is the capacity to be alone in the presence of someone (mother, lover, other). Playing is always a creative experience. Playing takes place on the theoretical line between the subjective and that which is objectively perceived. So, from transitional phenomena through playing to cultural especially creative experiences. In play we are free to be creative and creative activity is ultimately the search for the self. As Rollo May argues in *Man's Search for Himself*, just as only in playing is communication possible, so it is only in being creative that the individual discovers the self. Creativity is one way of being-in-the-world. The opposite of creativity is compliance (what Frankl calls conformism).

"On the seashore of endless worlds, children play." — Tagore

The sea and the shore symbolize intercourse and the child emerges from such sexual union. Indeed, we are only alone in the presence of someone. Frankl says there is one thing needed more than sexual intimacy and that is existential privacy. We must have the courage to be lonely. The transitional object is a symbol of the first experience of play. This play area is what life is about. The absence of a psychoneurotic illness may be health, but it is not life. Cultural experiences are in direct relationship with play, the play of those who have not yet heard of games. The emotionally deprived child is unable to play and has an impoverished capacity of experience in the cultural field. Creativity is a derivative of play. *Three* factors can be highlighted:

- Inner psychic reality
- Outer world of reality
- Transitional space (the in-between)

Play thus expands into creative living and the whole cultural life of humanity. This third space is the third way of living, the mystical space somewhere between behavior and contemplation, action and thought: a lucid dream. It is the task of the young to teach grown-ups to see "the newness that is in every stale thing when we look at it as children."[6]

---

6. A line from Patrick Kavanagh's poem, "Advent." See Kavanagh, *Complete Poems*.

Creative Thinking

Creativity is the key to solving problems and good decision-making—the ability to think both analytically and creatively. Creativity sparks innovation and innovation is based on improvisation. Yes, analysis is important in the decision-making process, but one needs to infuse it with imagination. Creative thinking can assist in identifying the strongest solution. It can renew motivation, promote clarity and positivity, strengthen critical thinking, help us see the big picture, and crank up productivity. Schools and society can rob us of our creative confidence. Education has become a tool of mass destruction, deadening, and dampening down a child's innate imagination, intuition, and intelligence. A creative mindset can be applied to almost all aspects of life, including decision-making. Creativity is ultimately a way of seeing. In *The Art of Creative Thinking*, Rod Judkins outlines some suggestions:

- Always be a beginner (do things in a new way)
- Cultivate your talents (innate) and skills (learned) to unleash your creative potential
- Do not be someone else, just be yourself
- Do something that matters to you—follow your passion or your purpose ("the bliss of being")

> "The least of things with a meaning are worth more in life than the greatest of things without it."—C. G. Jung

- Be committed, inventive
- Be positive about negatives
- Put your personality before your practicality
- Do not think about what others think about
- Be naturally inspired (nature is creative by necessity) rather than expired
- Find the work that for you is play
- Get into what you are into
- Grow old without growing up

Dynamics of Discernment

- If it ain't broke, break it
- Pick yourself up (10 percent of life is what happens to you, 90 percent is decided by how you respond to what happens to you. Attitude is more important than ability).
- Embrace competition
- Leave an indelible impression (it is not what you see, it is about what you make others see)
- Make a difference (Steve Jobs did a calligraphy course at college not a computer course. Richard Branson started out not knowing the difference between net and gross profit)
- Be mature enough to be childlike (it is the child in you who is creative not the adult in you)
- Maintain mountain—stick to something. Stay the course
- Make the present a present (the meaning of the moment)

"Real generosity towards the future lies in giving all to the present."—Albert Camus

- Open your mind and heart
- Pause for thoughtlessness
- Plan to have more accidents
- If you fail, fail again, just better (Winston Churchill: "Success is the ability to go from failure to failure without losing your enthusiasm")
- Work the hours that work for you (routine is mindless repetition)
- Put the right thing in the wrong place (see differently. André Breton: "The man who can't visualize a horse galloping on a tomato is an idiot")
- Stay hungry (luxury is a motivational sedative)
- Surprise yourself (do something new)
- Take advantage of a disadvantage—the obstacle is the opportunity
- Stay curious (the cure for boredom is curiosity; fortunately, there is no cure for curiosity)

- Find balance in your work-life
- Make it memorable (in other words, make it meaningful)
- Be an experiment
- Embrace opportunities (in other words, say yes to life in spite of everything)
- Cross-pollinate
- Stay playful (Heraclitus: "Man is most himself when he achieves the seriousness of a child at play")
- Get out of your mind
- Box your way out of boxes
- To learn, teach
- Be radical or redundant
- Make a mark—leave a legacy

For Viktor Frankl, creativity is one path to meaningful living. Too much thinking—what he calls "hyperreflection"—is a severe handicap to creativity and decision-making. Creations and decisions emerge from the spiritual unconscious. Frankl exhorts us to move into the realm of meaning and order our lives to nature, culture, and art.[7] Imagination is the fountainhead of human experience. Rollo May, the existential psychologist, talks about the "courage to create" and distinguishes the following types of courage:[8]

- Physical
- Moral
- Social
- Creative

Courage is ontological (*coeur* = heart). Every creative encounter is a new event, and every time requires another assertion of courage. Creative artists give birth to some new reality, enlarging human consciousness.

---

7. Frankl, *On the Theory*, 32–33, 36, 206–13.
8. See May, *Courage to Create*.

Dynamics of Discernment

The Creative Process

Let us look at the creative process itself:

- The creative act is an *encounter*—artists encounter the landscape they paint and are absorbed by it. They are in a "flow" state of *aesthetic arrest*. There is an *engagement*.
- There is an intensity to this engaged encounter. The artist (creative, deciding person) is caught up in it. He feels joy (his source many be nonconscious—it is not irrational, more suprarational). He "abandons" himself to it, through heightened awareness. It brings intellectual, volitional, and emotional functions into play all together. The dichotomy between subject and object is blurred. The world and self are in dialectical interplay.

Creativity is the encounter of the intensively conscious human being with the world. Creative people will frequently say "the idea dawned on me." The breakthrough comes from a depth below consciousness. The characteristics of the breakthrough experiences are:

- *Suddenness* of the insight or illumination
- The insight occurs against what one has clung to consciously
- There is a *vividness* to the incident and the scene that surrounds it
- There is *brevity* and conciseness to the insight and an immediate experience of *certainty*
- *Hard work* has been carried out on a topic *prior* to the breakthrough
- There is a *rest* in which the unconscious work proceeds on its own
- There is the necessity of alternating work and relaxation

Such creativity emerging from the subliminal self exhibits a purposiveness without purpose and enlarges the meaning of our lives. The creative artist is priest, prophet, and poet, is a menace to cultural conformity with his "free creativity." As such, he witnesses to the possibility of revelation. The creative person plays with ideas. This playing is an encounter in which anxiety is temporarily suspended, bracketed, halted.

We can all try to become more creative with our decisions—to see them in an artistic light, as a poet might view them. The Delphic Oracle was really a therapist whom the Greeks visited. This beautiful shrine was situated in a long valley stretching between massive mountain ranges and the deep blue-green sea of the Bay of Corinth. Here, Apollo gave counsel through his Pythian priestesses, as we mentioned at the beginning of this book. The shrine was a concrete expression of symbols and myths which embodied ritual, so important in creative decision-making. The creative decision-maker stands on the threshold (the liminal space) between possibility and necessity. Imagination outreaches the mind and brings true joy from our participation in being itself. Of course, creative art can form as much as deform, both reveal and conceal being. Plato calls this making of meaning Eros—love itself.

Insight

According to Jesuit philosopher Bernard Lonergan, insight, which is a dramatic instance of a revealed truth, possesses the following characteristics:

- It comes as a release to the tension of enquiry
- It comes suddenly and unexpectedly
- It is a function not of outer circumstances but inner conditions
- It pivots between the concrete and the abstract
- It passes into the habitual texture of one's mind[9]

> "Deep within us all, emergent when the noise of other appetites is stilled, there is a drive to know, to understand, to see why, to discover the reason, to find the cause, to explain," Bernard Lonergan

Insight depends on a perpetual alertness, ever asking the little question "why?"; from darkness to increasing light; from clues to the concept; from questioning to the creative decision. The "why?" comes from wonder, the desire to understand which is the beginning of all wisdom. We can discern *four* moments:

- The *awakening* of the intelligence (which releases us from the dominance of the biological drive)
- The *hint* (or suggestion—we must be on the right track)
- The *process* (imagination has been released from other cares)

9. See Lonergan, *Insight*.

- The *achievement* (here insight, image, and concept present a solid front)

Image, question, insight, and concept combine. There is, of course, the *inverse insight*—here the point is that there is no point, the solution is to deny a solution. If imagination is the playground of our desires, so conception is the playground of our intelligence. The image is necessary for the insight. Insight is the act of catching on to a connection. Intelligibility is the content of an insight. Insights enable us to abstract, in other words, to grasp the essential, to disregard the incidental, to see what is significant and to set aside the irrelevant.

The term "eureka effect" refers to this common experience of suddenly understanding a problem which appeared indissoluble. It gives rise to an "aha" moment, an insight or epiphany. There are *four* defining attributes of this AHA experience:

- The aha moment appears *suddenly*
- The *solution* to a problem can now proceed smoothly and fluently
- The aha moment elicits *positive affect*
- A person experiencing the aha moment is *convinced* that a solution is true

Insight is a two-phase process: In the first phase of an aha experience the problem-solver comes upon an impasse; he is stuck; encounters a stumbling block. The solution does not appear. In the second phase something occurs unexpectedly, after a break in mental function, and the answer is retrieved. To solve the problem, to make a creative decision, we need to think outside the box, or not to think.

Genius

Genius is creative. The term genius tends to be attributed to a person who displays exceptional insight or ability, creative productivity, or originality. The word "genius" is derived from *genie*—the guiding spirit of a person. There are, of course, various ways to assess intelligence. How do you measure a Mozart or a Leonardo da Vinci with a psychometric test? Immanuel Kant maintained that genius is the ability to arrive independently at and understand concepts that would normally have to be taught.

Aha: The Eureka Effect

We can relate a story about the ancient Greek polymath, Archimedes (circa 250 BC). Archimedes was asked by the local king to determine whether a crown was pure gold. During a trip to a public bath, Archimedes noted that water was displaced when his body sank into the bath and that the volume of water displaced equaled the volume of his body immersed in the water. He discovered a way to measure the volume of an irregular object. He leaped out naked, crying "eureka"—"I have found it," and allegedly ran through the streets of Syracuse elated, transported with joy. There would be no lightbulbs or candles or sandwiches without an insight. And then someone *deciding* to bring this idea into outer action. If it takes creativity to experience it, it takes courage to express it.

There can be a eureka *experience* and not just a eureka *effect*. Experience is the mastery gained through involvement or exposure. The history of the word "experience" aligns closely with the concept of *experiment*. Experience refers to mentally unprocessed, immediately perceived events and to the purported wisdom gained in reflection on and interpretation of them. Different types of experience include physical (environment), mental (intellectual), emotions, spiritual, social, visceral etc. There are first-hand experiences (you hear people often saying "you had to be there"), second-hand experiences (summarized from first-hand experiences), or third-hand experiences (unreliable rumor or hearsay). Decide what this means: "The haystack was important because the cloth ripped." Clue: parachute. *Two* theories have been put forward in relation to how people solve insight problems:

- Progress monitoring theory

Analyze the distance from their current position to the desired effect (from state to goal). Once they realize they cannot solve the problem while on their current path they will seek alternative solutions.

- Representational change theory

Here a person uses inappropriate knowledge as they set unnecessary constraints upon the problem. Once the person relaxes his constraints they can try and sort it out.

Dynamics of Discernment

In scientific terms, functional magnetic resonance imaging discovered that problem-solving requiring insight involves increased activity in the right cerebral hemisphere. Some unconscious processing may take place during sleep; discoveries can be made in dreams. For example, the ring structure of benzene came to Von Stradonitz in a dream when a snake was eating its own tail. Sleep allows for unconscious thought to break through. When an impasse occurs, a change in attitude is needed. Question: What is the thing that can move heavy logs, but cannot move a small nail? Answer: a river. Question: A man was washing windows on a high-rise building when he fell from the 40-feet adder to the concrete path below. Amazingly, he was unhurt. Why? Answer: he slipped from the bottom rung. Question: Make a word from PIOHP. Answer HIPPO.

Examples of the aha effect include scientific discoveries made after a certain flash of inspiration/intuition/illumination/insight such as Einstein's special theory of relativity, which occurred to him as he was talking to a friend. Alec Jeffreys was in his lab looking at the X-ray film image of a DNA experiment at 9.05 am on Monday Sept 10th, 1984. He realized the scope of DNA profiling within 30 minutes.

In terms of creative problem-solving, different techniques have been proposed, such as cognitive reframing—changing one's focus, and brainstorming—as well as multiple ideas facilitation.

Some Examples

On September 28th, 1931 at the age of 33, C. S. Lewis got into his brother's motorcycle (sidecar) to travel to a zoo near London. "When we set out, I did not believe that Jesus Christ is the son of God, and when we reached the zoo I did." He likened it to awakening, with no great emotion, from a long sleep. He then decided to become a Christian and lived out the rest of his life as a committed Anglican.[10]

Moses "saw" God in a burning bush and replied "Yes, I am here." He was told, "Take off your sandals. The place where you stand is holy ground." His subsequent decisions were all made in the light of this epiphany.

St. Augustine prayed under a fig tree and heard a child chanting, "pick it up and read." He interpreted this as a divine command and read from the Bible this passage: "not in riots and drunken parties, not in eroticism,

---

10. This Lewis anecdote is referenced in Irvine, *Aha!*, 23. See also Lewis, *Surprised by Joy*.

nor in strife, but put on the Lord Jesus Christ and make no provisions for the flesh." The change was instant and profound. "A light of relief from all anxiety flooded my heart" and, like Moses, his decisions after would be imbued with the light of divine radiance. These historical personages experienced conversions, epiphanies. Spiritually speaking, they can be interpreted as visions, psychiatrically as hallucinations. It depends on the differential diagnosis. Was Joan of Arc a saint or a schizophrenic? 2+2=4 even when a schizophrenic says it! Ezekiel, who was subject to visions and inner locutions, was also an epileptic, as was Dostoyevsky.

The Overview Effect

The term "overview effect" is a term employed by some astronauts to describe the cognitive shift in their awareness that occurs during spaceflight after viewing Earth from outer space. They reported that after returning to earth, everything changed. Of course, there is the "bandwagon effect" whereby belief begets additional belief. Mohandas Gandhi experienced racial discrimination in South Africa in 1893 when he was thrown off a train despite having a first-class ticket. Later, he would emerge as a world-famous civil rights leader (*Mahatma* in Sanskrit means "great soul"). Sometimes such moral or religious aha moments emerge as a response to a traumatic event—transformations are triggered, and all decisions afterwards come seamlessly from these transpersonal experiences, which pose a challenge to ordinary ways of being. Plato tells us that early one morning Socrates was thinking about something that was niggling him and would not give up but continued thinking from early dawn until noon—standing there, immobile, lost in thought, and with the return of light he offered up a prayer and went on his way. What was he doing? He was engaged in sustained, focused, silent concentration, perhaps in dialogue with his inner *daimon* (conscience/spirit/Self). His was a life spent searching for the divine. Einstein similarly had a breakthrough with his general theory of relativity. He relates: "I was sitting on a chair in my patent office in Bern. Suddenly a thought struck me. If a man falls freely, he would not feel his weight. I was taken aback. This simple thought experiment made a deep impression on me. This led me to the theory of gravity." He described it as "the happiest thought in my life." (It took him a further eight years to work it out). Roger Penrose, the mathematical physicist, reported in the 1960s that an idea came to him as he crossed the street, which added substantially

Dynamics of Discernment

to our knowledge of black holes in the universe. In 1979, Alan Guth woke at 1 am and wrote in a piece of paper "spectacular realization"—about the Big Bang. The idea came to be known as the inflationary universe theory. Now, these are *big* rather than *banal* insights about the nature of the universe. They are insights into the truth of things. There can be anti-aha-moments (inverse insights), as we said, when you realize that you have made a mistake about something. These moments contribute just as much to advances as aha moments do. There seems to be in the cases cited above a collaboration between the conscious and nonconscious mind. The former is rule-bound and linear, the latter lateral and playfully creative. Conscious effort is a necessary but not sufficient condition for attaining an aha moment. Usually, after which, there is ecstatic joy in discovery as, for example, in the description Freud gave it: "the incomparable pleasure of gaining first insight." James Watson and Francis Crick, who discovered the structure of DNA, marched into the Eagle pub at lunch time and announced that they had "just discovered the secret of life." Curiosity (marvel) motivated these men, what Lonergan calls, following Aristotle, "an unrestricted desire to know."[11] Their minds were open, enquiring, amenable to reason, unlike the British public who, as Oscar Wilde quipped, has "an insatiable curiosity to know everything, except what is worth knowing."[12] Later, these individuals would enlist others in terms of cooperation, what Lonergan calls "functional collaboration."[13] Sometimes, the world was not ready for their announcements and their revelations would be routinely rejected (example, the Galileo affair). Of course, we might also get little "ahas." These do not come to us as thunderbolts out of the blue. Orhan Pamuk, a Nobel laureate in literature, tells of rewriting the first line of a novel 50–100 times. Successful writers are almost always rewriters (writing involves lots of deleting and discarding). Hemingway put it thus: "the best of a book is how much good stuff you can throw away."[14] The composer James Mobberley said that 2 percent of his time is spent coming up with an idea and that the other 98 percent is spent reworking and extending the idea. Sometimes artists have attempted to induce inspiration through psychotropics/psychedelics—to manage their muse. There is a term called the "knickerbocker rule" named

---

11. Lonergan, *Insight*, 97.

12. Irvine, *Aha!*, 147.

13. Functional collaboration is a concept found throughout Lonergan, *Method in Theology*.

14. Irvine, *Aha!*, 276.

Creativity

after Conrad Knickerbocker who was a newspaper owner and author of fiction. He was once asked by one of his employees how he could become a "real" writer, to which he answered: "You apply ass to chair"! In other words, to become a writer you must spend a lot of time actually writing! To give some examples: Flaubert worked 7 hours a day, Joseph Conrad worked 8 hours a day, Somerset Maugham worked 4 hours a day, and Ernest Hemingway worked 6 hours a day. Some writers such as Vladimir Nabokov wrote on index cards; Balzac required coffee; others needed music or mood enhancing drugs; others benefitted from solitude and silence. (Plato speaks of "the madness of the Muses").

Epiphany

We have mentioned epiphany above a few times. An epiphany may be defined as a sudden realization or revelation. If it comes, all our decisions flow with an inner certainty and conviction—they are carried along seamlessly. The word epiphany derives from the Greek for "manifestation" or "striking appearance." The term is generally used to describe any scientific breakthrough or philosophical discovery, but it can be applied to any situation which leads to an attitudinal alteration/adjustment. Epiphany originally referred to insight through the divine. Its secular usage owes much to James Joyce, who deployed it as a literary device within each entry of his short story collection *Dubliners*. His protagonists come to sudden recognitions that change their view of themselves. Joyce first expounded an epiphany's meaning in the fragment "Stephen Hero," although this was published posthumously in 1944. For philosopher Emmanuel Lévinas, epiphany is a manifestation of the Absolute as seen in another's face, this face of the Other who orders and ordains us, this face as trace for the absent One.[15] Culturally, rites and initiations and mystery religions as well as the arts have served as vehicles of everyday epiphanies. They come in different forms and are generated by a complex combination and confluence of experience, memory, knowledge, and context. They come as a pleasant surprise; they cannot be predicted or controlled. In 1905 while taking a streetcar home and trying to reconcile Newtonian physics and Maxwell's equations, Einstein looked behind him at the receding clock tower in Bern and realized that if the car sped up close to the speed of light, he would see

---

15. Lévinas uses this notion of "face" througout his writings. See especially *Totality and Infinity*.

Dynamics of Discernment

the clock slow down. About this thought, he later remarked: "a storm broke loose in my mind"—one which would allow him to understand special relativity. Two years later, he experienced another epiphany which he called "the happiest thought of my life," when he imagined an elevator falling and realized that a passenger would not be able to tell the difference between the weightlessness of falling and the weightlessness of space—a thought which allowed him to generalize his theory of relativity to include gravity as a curvature in spacetime.[16] Charles Darwin, for his part, said he had a "hunch" about natural selection and later that he remembered the spot on the road where his carriage was when he had the epiphany. In Christianity, the Epiphany refers to a realization that Christ is the Son of God (the feast celebrated on January 6 is the visit of the Magi or three wise men from the East). Another example would be the Buddha attaining enlightenment under the bodhi tree. In Zen, the term *kensho* us deployed to describe the moment when one realizes the answer to a koan.

It is worth noting two more complementary concepts: "inscape" and "instress," which are employed by Jesuit poet Gerard Manley Hopkins, and derived from Duns Scotus, the Mediaeval Franciscan philosopher, to describe individuality and the uniqueness of persons and things ("thisness"). Hopkins felt that everything in the universe was characterized by *inscape*—that distinctive divine design that constitutes individual identity. Each being in the universe "selves," that is to say, enacts its unique identity. The human is the most highly selved and recognizes the inscape of other beings in an act that Hopkins calls *instress*, an apprehension of an object in an intense thrust of energy toward it that enables one to realize specific distinctness.[17] Ultimately, the instress of inscape leads to Christ (*imago Dei*). Thomas Merton, who was influenced by both Hopkins and Duns Scotus, equates the thingness of a thing—its inscape—to sanctity. Holiness is thus grounded in God's creation (incarnation) and not in a Platonic (other-worldly) ideal.[18]

To enjoy an epiphany is to experience the mystical in the mundane, the ultimate in the ordinary, to see the sacral in the carnal, "The Father through the features of men's faces" as Hopkins puts it. In *As Kingfishers Catch Fire*, Hopkins describes it thus:

> Each mortal thing does one thing and the same:

16. Irvine, *Aha!*, 129.
17. See Hopkins, *As Kingfishers Catch Fire*.
18. See Horan, *Franciscan Heart*.

Creativity

> Deals out that being indoors each one dwells;
>
> Selves—goes itself;
>
> myself it speaks and spells,
>
> Crying what I do is me: for that I came.

This "poor potsherd patch" is "immortal diamond" (Hopkins). In the "foul rag and bone shop of the heart" (Yeats), flesh finds its forever and the "Leafy-with-love banks" pour redemption (Patrick Kavanagh's theo-poetics): epiphany as eschatology.[19]

Inspiration

Creative inspiration rests on inner sight, which is always new, fresh. It is like a spark leaping off a fire and enlivening the soul. It is reputed that Mozart, for example, held all the musical notes in his mind. He heard them "all at once." He opined, "When I am, as it were, completely myself, entirely alone, and of good cheer . . . it is on such occasions that my ideas flow best and most abundantly. Whence and how they come I know not, nor can I force them."[20] All of us are artists. It matters not *what* we do but *how* we do it—we can sweep streets like a Shakespeare. There is one mind common to all—the Self-same—and art is the appearance or epiphany of this cosmic consciousness. Just as Shakespeare wrote wisdom, so did Michelangelo paint wisdom, and Beethoven compose wisdom. All creativity and all beauty are owed to the ultimate Artist, the Absolute. It is said about Michelangelo's statue of David that he did not put David into the stone, rather, he simply took everything out of the stone that was not David. Art takes us from forms to the formless, from sounds to silence, from activity to stillness, and from beautiful objects to Beauty itself. Art points, gestures in the direction of the transcendental. The ego limits creativity as much as decision-making. When the ego discriminates, we cannot see objectively; we are locked into solipsistic subjectivity. The ego is full of frozen and false knowledge. We do not experience anything as it is. The still Self in everyone, by contrast, conserves energy, creates anew. When the ego disappears, the Self manifests and inspires. If the ego is mechanical and repetitive,

---

19. I have here weaved together bits from three famous poems: Gerard Manley Hopkins, "That Nature is a Heraclitean Fire and of the Comfort of the Resurrection"; William Butler Yeats, "The Circus Animal's Desertion"; and Patrick Kavanagh, "Canal Bank Walk."

20. Holmes, *Life of Mozart*, 329.

the Self is creative, inspirational, conscious, and receptive. These are the conditions conducive to create decision-making. Ego-lessness is the ideal state. When we are receptive, we always obtain the message intended for us by the universe, which is creative by nature. Creativity and decision-making are ultimately nothing to do with our individuality and everything to do with our universality (*samashti*). Both involve surrendering to a power not our own, and harnessing its vast energy. Creativity is an allowing, not a doing. The song of the soul does not come *from* us, it comes *through* us. We are but instruments, conduits of consciousness. There is no aim in art, no goal, only letting go, release. Certain techniques only serve the creativity, just as they do the decision-making. When one rises to the highest level of consciousness, one finds pure creativity, decisions without the decision making. Just as an artist needs a blank canvas to paint, so do we require a *tabula rasa* (empty slate). Then we do not look at the flower; it looks at us. Art approximates to the Absolute. In losing ourselves in the activity, we find our Self, for the universe intends to manifest something through us. All insights and the best decisions based on unshakeable foundations emanate from the still mind. If you agitate water, you cannot see into the water; if there is much movement the dirt will be churned up. To be creative and to make good decisions requires one thing: not to think your way into a solution but to still yourself for a solution. Receptivity rather than retention is the key to both: meditation as the master-key that unlocks true creative decision-making.

"Creativity is intelligence having fun."—Albert Einstein

4

Applying Theory U

"Theory U" is Otto Scharmer's 2006 change-management model.[1] With his colleagues at MIT, he conducted 150 interviews with entrepreneurs and innovators in business, science, and society, and then extended the basic strands into a theory of learning. Scharmer argues that our capacity to pay attention co-shapes the world. What prevents us from so doing is that we are not fully aware of that inner condition from which our attention and actions originate. These blind spots need to be illuminated. In this chapter we adduce the process, principles, and practices of Theory U—it is a framework which can effectively be applied to decision-making. In short, it is a system for implementing awareness-based change. We have to cultivate the soil of the social field—of thinking, conversing, deciding, organizing. This source will affect the quality of listening, learning, and leading. The power of intention is highlighted as the source of curiosity, compassion, and courage. The shift is from *ego*-system to *eco*-system awareness, from a silo to a systems' perspective, one that has the well-being of all at its heart (*chitta*). Why this is important is because *energy follows attention*.

Scharmer begins by mentioning the *three* great divides:

- The *ecological* divide—environmental destruction
- The *social* divide—levels of inequality

---

1. I am much in debt to Scharmer, *The Essentials of Theory U*, which is a helpful encapsulation of Scharmer's change-management model. This entire chapter is somewhat of a summary and commentary on Scharmer's work.

Dynamics of Discernment

- The *spiritual* divide—loss of meaning and contact with the Self (as distinct from the ego, with the former referring to one's highest potential, in Scharmer's language)

Any successful intervention to bring about transformational change will depend on the *inner* condition of the intervener. The first divide is a disconnect between self and nature; the social divide arises from a disconnect between self and other; while the spiritual divide results from a disconnect between self and Self. Scharmer's objective is to get us to presence our potential. His word is "presencing"—blending "sensing" with "presence".

Form follows consciousness. Things emerge from what I attend to. Mindfulness is the practice of paying attention to our attention, just as dialogue is the capacity of a system to see itself. Theory U attempts to make a system sense and see itself: from surface to source. There are different levels of action: envisioning, enacting, embodying. The *three* movements in any process (for example, decision-making) will be:

- Observe (witness)
- Retreat (reflect)
- Prototype (acting from what emerges in the naked now)

These are *three* gestures of becoming aware: suspension (of habitual patterns), redirection (of attention from exterior to interior, from object to mind), and letting go. Scharmer suggests *seven* ways of attending to the world:

- Downloading—our old mental habits and familiar patterns of behavior (same old).
- Seeing—when we suspend our habitual judgement, we notice the new and see the world afresh.
- Sensing—when we redirect our attention from objects to source, our perception widens and deepens; the boundary between observer and observed opens up.
- Presencing—entering into stillness, we let go (surrender) the old and connect with future possibilities.
- Crystallizing—vision clarifies, and envisioning happens from the field of the future (rather than from our ego).
- Prototyping—here we enact and explore by doing (action).

- Performing—here we embody the new by evolving our practices and infrastructures, from the context of the bigger frame of reference/larger eco-system.

All seven performances may be applied to our decision-making processes.

Three Instruments

Observe, retreat, act. The *three* instruments of inner knowing are:

- *Open mind* (the capacity to suspend old habits of judgement and to see with fresh eyes)
- *Open heart* (the capacity to empathize and look at the situation through the eyes of another)
- *Open will* (the capacity to let go of the old and welcome in the new)

These three contemplative practices are essential for wise and conscious decision-making.

Four Types of Listening

What is essential throughout any process, including decision-making, is *listening*, of which there are *four* archetypes:

- *Habitual* listening—limited to reconfirming what we already know (from my past experiences).
- *Factual* listening—we let the data speak to us and notice disconfirming information (from my open mind).
- *Empathic* listening—we see the situation through the eyes of another (from my open heart).
- *Generative* listening—we listen out for the highest future potential and possibility to show up while holding a space for something new to be born (from my open will).

In level 1, your attention is not focused on what the other person is saying but on your own inner commentary. As you cross from level 1 to 2, your attention moves from listening to your inner voice to actually listening to your interlocutor. When you cross the threshold from factual to empathic listening (level 2 to 3), your place of listening shifts from you to

Dynamics of Discernment

the other person, from the intelligence of your head to the intelligence of your heart. Finally, when you move from empathic to generative listening (level 3 to 4), your listening becomes a holding space for something new to come into reality. We can apply these shifts in consciousness to our decision-making powers/prowess. However, the three gates we cross are guarded by three enemies or voices of resistance.

The Three Voices

- Voice of Judgement (VoJ)
- Voice of Cynicism (VoC)
- Voice of Fear (VoF)

These voices can stop any decision in its tracks. The first enemy blocks the gate to the open mind, the second to the open heart, and the third to the open will. Firstly, the critical starting point is to suspend one is your judgmental voice because this voice shuts down the power of the creative mind. Secondly, we must make ourselves vulnerable/humble. Thirdly, we need to dissolve our fear of loss. Interestingly, leadership derives from *leith* meaning "to go forth" or "cross the threshold" or "to die." Putting it another way, the three enemies, which result in "absencing" (abrogating in decision-making) are:

- Ignorance—the closing of the mind
- Hate—the closing of the heart
- Fear—the closing of the will

By contrast, the cycle of "presencing" is based on:

- Curiosity—the opening of the mind
- Compassion—the opening of the heart
- Courage—the opening of the will

Once we have crossed the threshold, we face *two* main challenges.

Two Barriers

- Mindless action

- Action-less mind

If in mindless action we implement ideas or make decisions without any learning having taken place, in action-less mind, paralysis stops us prototyping; we discuss things to death. Both are to be avoided.

Four Types of Action

There are *four* fundamental forms of action:

- Attending (micro)
- Conversing (meso)
- Organizing (macro)
- Coordinating (mundo)

If these four constitute the social field, the *four* structures of attention are the ways in which action and attention enter the world. They are:

- Habitual: decisions based on past experiences (I-in-me)
- Ego-system: new noticings (I-in-it)
- Empathic-relational: the viewpoint of others (I-in-you)
- Generative eco-system: flow (I-in-us)

Every social action emerges from one of these four sources/structures of attention. The way I pay attention shapes how the social reality around me unfolds. We need thus to cultivate our attention, especially when it comes to big decision-making. When you apply a flame to a piece of metal, nothing happens at first but after a while the metal changes states from solid to fluid. The same happens in conversations—they drop to a deeper level when one attends. Scharmer distinguishes *four* different stages or qualities of conversation:

- Downloading (operating at the level of polite and platitudinous chat): Bubble
- Debate (here people speak their minds or brainstorming occurs): Adaptive
- Dialogue (from *logos*, "word" and *dia*, "through," so "meaning moving through"): Reflective

Dynamics of Discernment

- Collective creativity (presencing—time slowing down, space opening up, decentering): Generative

Organizations structure our collective decision making. There are *four* different stages in the evolution of organizations:

- Centralized—here decision-making power is placed at the top of the pyramid
- Decentralized—the power is closer to the periphery; independence prevails
- Networked—structures are flattened; rise of networking relationships
- Eco-system—connectivity; shared purpose; decision-making is pushed further to the frontline; empowerment

As we move from level 1 to 4, there is a gradual *opening* of mind, heart, and will, and a progressive *deepening* of the intelligence.

- Conforming—habitual—rule-repeating—from habitual patterns
- Confronting—rational—rule-realizing—from the head
- Connecting—relational—rule-reflecting—from the heart
- Collective—emerging (higher Self)—rule-generating—from the whole

Scharmer suggests that we drop everything that is not essential (as we negotiate the eye of the needle—this is the narrow gate) and begin to see ourselves from a higher vantage point (what I call the Big Picture). This involves letting go of ego (ego is not our amigo), and stepping instead into the spaciousness of the Self. Here, we listen to ourselves, others, and to what is emerging from the source/Self. Below, are some principles Scharmer sets out:

- Practice deep listening and dialogue with open mind and heart
- Listen to what life calls you to do (as Frankl puts it: life asks something of us)[2]
- Dialogue with interesting players on the edges
- Clarify core questions

---

2. Frankl repeats something like this in several places. See especially Frankl, *Man's Search*.

- Convene a diverse group around a shared intention
- Trust your heart's intelligence
- Observe
- Suspend your voice of judgement
- Connect with a sense of wonder
- Integrate heart, head, and hand

Accessing creativity/creative decision-making and problem-solving as well as creating a learning environment both coalesce around *two* questions:

>Who is my Self?

>What is my Work?

On these two rotates the axis of the world, and they are best carried out in: **Nature** and in **Silence**. At its core, the process involves presencing. The words *essence*, *presence*, and *present* (gift) all share the same Indo-European root-word "*sat*" meaning "truth" and "goodness." It also means avoiding deciding without learning (mindless action), analysis paralysis (action-less mind), and talking without embodied change (blah-blah-blah; empty speech). When considering evolving an idea for prototyping or making a decision, ask these *seven* questions.

The Seven Rs

- Is it *relevant*?
- Is it *revolutionary*?
- Is it *rapid*?
- Is it *rough*?
- Is it *right*?
- Is it *relationally* effective?
- Is it *replicable*?

Theory U aims to be a framework, a method, and a movement, one which supports salutogenesis rather than maintaining pathogenesis: from an emphasis, in other words, on what is wrong (illness) to an emphasis on what is right (wellness), as we seek to create a space at the intersection

Dynamics of Discernment

of science, spirituality, and social change, one which will link the intelligences of the three centers of body (gut), mind, and heart. Whatever way we approach it, Theory U can help with better and wiser decisions. What makes the template so attractive is that its language and logistics are in marked agreement/congruence with the content of the previous chapters: substance and style converge in synergy.

5

Synchronicity

I Ching

IN THIS CHAPTER, WE will examine two so-called divinatory tools for decision-making and how retrieving them through synchronicity can help with creative and intuitive decision-making.

The *I Ching*, also known as the *Book of Changes*, is an ancient Chinese manual which has been used for divination and personal decision-making purposes for 3,000 years. It has been consulted down the centuries by Emperors and ordinary people alike intent on getting guidance and wisdom from this Oriental oracle for their small and big decisions. Dating from the Zhou dynasty of 1000–750 BC, it has become a classic cosmological text with a series of philosophical commentaries accompanying it, informed by Confucianism, Taoism, and Buddhism. It is one of the most famous books in the world, a foundational text for Eastern philosophical traditions which attracted the interest in the West of Enlightenment intellectuals. G. W. Leibnitz, the philosopher, (who was corresponding with the Jesuits in China at the time) penned the first European commentary on it in 1703. His interpretation was critiqued by G. W. Hegel, and Jacques Derrida (father of deconstruction) in the twentieth century follows on in the wake of Hegel, maintaining that the Chinese language cannot express philosophical ideas. After the revolution of 1911, the *I Ching* was no longer part of mainstream Chinese philosophy, but parallels were made between it and algebra as well as logic in computer science. C. G. Jung took an interest in its imagery and

Dynamics of Discernment

introduced an influential German translation by Richard Wilhelm, introducing his own theories from analytical psychology such as archetypes (ordering patterns of behavior) and synchronicity (a non-coincidental correspondence between two apparently unrelated sequences of events). The *I Ching* had a notable impact on 1960s counterculture, especially with the literary set, such as Hermann Hesse. It has been translated dozens of times, the one into Latin having taken place in the 1730s and carried out by a French Jesuit missionary. But the most influential modern translation was the 1923 version by Richard Wilhelm, which was translated into English (from the German) in 1950. At the core of its philosophy is the concept of permanent change. As Heraclitus remarked, all things are in constant flux and flow. The only permanent constant is the constancy of change itself.

Ideas are portrayed in the text itself as mountains and water and snakes and sun and fire. 8 trigrams are arranged in an octagonal shape comprising 8 (*ba*) areas (*guas*) or *Bakua*. Each *gua* has *yao* (line)-symbols consisting of 3 lines. Each line-symbol is either *yin* (feminine receptivity) or *yang* (masculine creativity). The 8 forces of change are: creativity, receptivity, boundlessness, consuming, obstruction, penetration, calmness, arousal. The confluence of these 8 forces drive the change of the universe and every situation/context of the human condition. Their interaction accounts for favorable and unfavorable outcomes for human personal and communal life. One does not read the hexagrams in sequence; there is no logical reason in the progression. One consults the *I Ching* according to the results of the coin toss. What is read will reflect and apply to your specific situation and concrete concerns. Jung regarded the hexagrams as archetypes—universal patterns pertaining to the collective unconscious. It is a treasure-trove of philosophical wisdom. The *I Ching* is divided into sixty-four thematic chapters, and each chapter is identified with a hexagram—a figure composed of six lines.

Synchronicity

The *I Ching* employs random numbers, six of which between 6 and 9 are turned into a hexagram. One consults the book and interprets what one reads—the symbolic material of the text.

There are 64 possible hexagrams, along with the hexagram name, short hexagram statement, and six-line statement. The *I Ching* is read as a microcosm of the universe that offers complex symbolic correspondences. Yin and Yang are represented by broken and solid lines. Yin is broken (—) while Yang is solid (_). It addresses 4,032 times 64, or 258,048 possible situations.

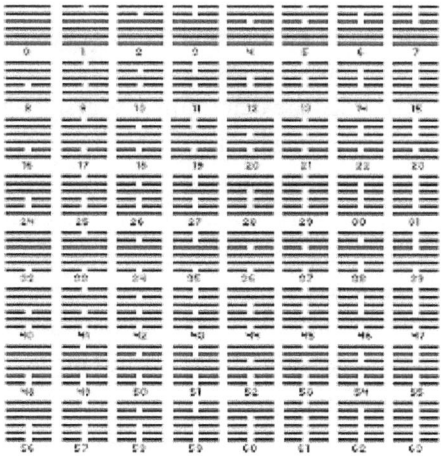

Steps:

- Frame the right question—be specific.

Dynamics of Discernment

- Shake the three identical coins and toss them to obtain the 6 *yao* (lines of your hexagram) six times. The first throw determines the base line and the sixth throw the top line. As you shake and toss the coins formulate a question and ask it interiorly.
- Identify the 6 lines of the obtained sequence.
- Consult the *I Ching*; read the description.

- 1st line: emotional assessment (of a situation)
- 2nd line: cognitive conscious evaluation for the situation
- 3rd line: conditions or circumstances of the situation
- 4th line: the attempt to take action (uncertainty of intended consequences)
- 5th line: the anticipated fully developed situation coming into its final favorable or unfavorable position
- 6th line: end of the process

It is not a game of chance. The 64 hexagram is an exhaustive set, representing "all there is," the whole situation. It is neither predictive nor prescriptive on the one hand, nor provisional and projective on the other hand. When guided by the *I Ching*, we begin to make sense of the events happening to us, receptive to reading the signs of the times. It is about how we read and receive the text.

The lines recorded are determined by assigning numerical values to heads and tails then adding the total. Each heads is 3, each tails is 2. So, if you cast one heads and two tails (3+2+2), you consult a 7. Toss the coins another five times recalling the numerical values and the corresponding line each time, building up your six-line hexagram from the bottom up. As you toss the coin, ask a question to the universe, for example: "Should I apply for the new job?" "Is it the right time to join this organization?" Or whatever it may be. Aside from the *I Ching* book, there are both free downloads and an App.

For Jung, the *I Ching* represents a door to the energy of the archetypes. *Tao* is the way; it suggests the interaction between mind (inner) and reality (outer). The *I Ching* points to an interdependence of events, and sees the subjective and objective as two aspects of the same reality. Mind, time, space, situation, action, and non-action are all intertwined. From this

Synchronicity

perspective, mind and matter are seen as interactive rather than independent and isolated. In *Memories, Dreams, Reflections*, Jung tells us he met Wilhelm in the 1920s, and in 1923 invited him to address the Psychology Club in Zurich on the *I Ching*. Jung informs us that before he met him, he was interested in "Oriental philosophy" and around the same time he began experimenting with the *I Ching* himself. He practiced the technique by referring the resultant oracles to one another in an interplay of question and answer. All sorts of "remarkable results" emerged—meaningful connections which he could not explain. The connection between the *psyche* and the physical worlds which Jung encountered was suggestive of an acausal parallelism which he would later call "synchronicity." A "significant" number of answers hit the mark. He gives the example of a young man who came to him with a strong mother complex who wished to marry after having met a young girl. However, he felt uncertain, fearing he might find himself under the influence/sway of his complex. (If complexes are hang-ups, synchronicities are heads-ups). Jung consulted the passage in the *I Ching*. It read: "The maiden is powerful. One should not marry such a maiden." He decided not to proceed with the marriage!

The *I Ching* is one of the oldest methods for grasping a situation as a whole—it comes in the form of a *gestalt*, and this against a cosmic background of the interplay between Yin and Yang. An equivalence of meaning between psychic states and physical processes, according to the Jungian formulation. The method of the *I Ching* and all divinatory techniques is intuitive and based on an acausal or synchronistic connective principle, which cannot be explained away as mere projection.

In my own case, after having tossed the coins and asking whether I should join a certain society, a Jungian colleague read the results out to me. I was rooted to the spot. It was so accurate and clear with the answer that I thought she was making it up and so I read the passage from the book myself. I was amazed. It confirmed I should join, which I did, and it proved a favorable move.

Synchronicity, which we will look at in a bit more detail below, is more about co-occurrence than coincidence. It calls upon two separate events occurring at a single moment and draws meaning from them even though there is no cause-and-effect between the events. In *Jung, Synchronicity, and Human Destiny*, Ira Progoff, the founder of the Intensive Journal Method, relates an experience he had using the *I Ching* with C. G. Jung in Switzerland. He handed Progoff three coins from his pocket and asked

Dynamics of Discernment

him what question he had. This event took place in Jung's garden beside the Lake of Zurich. Progoff tossed the coins and Jung noted the heads and tails and made the count. Jung recorded the 6 lines. The hexagram was formed and so the next step was to locate in the text of the *I Ching* the passage that corresponded to the hexagram. According to Progoff, the answer that it brought forth was "very meaningful." One of the paragraphs in question read: "Dispersion. Success. The king approaches his temple. It furthers one to cross the great waters. Perseverance furthers." It struck Progoff as "uncommonly relevant" to his specific situation, depicting, as it did, Progoff's trip over the waters from America to Europe to work with Jung and how that was having and would continue to have a beneficial effect on his personal and professional development. More images were given further on and Progoff employed Jung's method of amplification as well as active imagination to understand the symbolic material presented. Through the process and principle of "correlation," Progoff began to understand and appreciate the message. Neither chance nor causality, Progoff and Jung were convinced that the *I Ching* contained within itself a deep and subtle wisdom, offering instead a meaningful pattern of confluences, for those who had (hermeneutic) eyes to see.

The Tarot

> "There are many methods for developing the 'sense of symbols'.... One of the most interesting of these is the Tarot."—P. D. Ouspensky

Like the *I Ching*, the Tarot cards have also been deployed for divination, discernment, and decision-making. It too can be interpreted and deployed effectively and creatively via the principle of synchronicity and symbol-making.

> "The psyche consists essentially of images. It is a series of images in the truest sense, not an accidental juxtaposition or sequence, but a structure that is throughout full of meaning and purpose; it is a 'picturing of vital activities.'"—C. G. Jung

"Don't think, but look," wrote Ludwig Wittgenstein,[1] which implies, "Don't judge, but perceive." The Tarot involves looking, seeing-as. "Image

---

1. Wittgenstein, Philosophical Investigations, 66.

Synchronicity

is psyche," as C. G. Jung put it in his "Commentary on *The Secret of the Golden Flower*." According to Aristotle, "the soul never thinks without an image." Both the *I Ching* and Tarot have been used for strategic decision-making over the centuries, especially in times of change and crisis.

The major arcana of the Tarot are visual/imaginal aids to the unconscious. The Tarot introduces us to symbols and shapes, experienced synchronistically, which provides a window onto an alternative world. The cards are relics of a religious sensibility, an art gallery which have been perverted and sold as a fortune telling gimmick by occultists and necromancers (the "devil's pack"). But the Tarot is a system and school of spiritual exercises. There are Major and Minor Arcana. "*Arca*" in Latin means "chest"; "*arcere*" means "to shut" (our English word "arcane" comes from this root). So, it is suggestive of something secret. (Example: Noah's ark and the ark of the Covenant in the Hebrew Bible). The oldest pack of Tarot cards dates to fifteenth-century Italy. The earliest set is the Visconti-Sforza deck. (Francesco Sforza, the owner, died in 1466). Antoine Court de Gebelin—a French Protestant clergyman, archaeologist, and Freemason, held that the cards derived from 22 stones buried between the paws of the Sphinx which had been encoded by Egyptian priests to conceal esoteric doctrines. The use of them for divinatory purposes only began in eighteenth-century France. This high-jacking of the cards for cartomancy (so-called fortune or future-telling) spread from France to England and through the Order of the Golden Dawn spread throughout the world. The Order was responsible for the Ryder-Waite pack of Tarot cards. This version has been popular since the 1880s. The Marseilles Deck, by contrast, is symbolically striking and uncluttered. They depict icons, imbued with the imprint of theodicy and Christian soteriology. Playing cards was forbidden in 1369 in France. With the invention of printing and mass reproduction, over a million packs were printed in the 17th- century, three of which survive. In 1930, Paul Marteau produced the definitive edition—incorporating the best of all the diverse varieties in existence. These became known as "The Ancient Tarot of Marseilles." The major arcana, of which there are 22 cards, consists of inspiring images that may be used as a springboard to meditation and philosophical reflection on the mystery of life, as well as decision-making. They are works of art stemming from the creative, spiritual unconscious, and imbued with Western Christian iconography. They portray in symbolic form our inner reality and mark out a journey into psycho-spiritual wholeness. They possess an unknown origin, but experts argue that they are at least six centuries

Dynamics of Discernment

old. The Tarot Trumps narrate a symbolic story of the Self. If the ego is *made*; the Self is *given*. The best approach is to view them as you would paintings in an art-gallery. The Trumps are set out in sequence to form three horizontal rows of seven cards each.

The Tarot cards can be seen as a catalogue and projection holder, symbolically representing forces in the *psyche*, a veritable alphabet of archetypes, universal images, such as the archetypal mother, lover, fool, devil, trickster. The Tarot cards are a map of the deep, clues from the collective unconscious, visitors from inner space. We can read them psychologically and/or spiritually. We know the Tarot cards were used to play a game, similar to Bridge and popular in the sixteenth century. The pack consists of 56 cards—21 trump cards plus "the Fool" (so 22 major arcana). The name "tarot" comes from these "trump" cards—a French adaptation of the Italian "*tarocco*" (plural: *tarocchi*), previously referred to as "*cartes de trionfi*." "Triumph" (Latin: *triumphi*) became trump cards. The total number of Tarot cards is 78. Originally, as a game, one followed the suit that was played (suits were swords, clubs, cups, or coins rather than spades, clubs, hearts, and diamonds). If you had no card in the suit you could play the trump card. Points were awarded for each trick won.

The Tarot cards represent evocative images or symbols which portray in archetypal form an inner reality common to all of us (universal) yet peculiar to each of us at every moment of our lives (unique). The Rider-Waite pack issued from the Order of the Golden Dawn nearly replaced the Marseilles Deck. Arthur Edward Waite (1857–1942) was the publisher of the first set of Tarot cards in English. Pamela Colman Smith designed them, and Mary Hanson-Roberts colored them. Smith was deeply influenced by William Butler Yeats. Yeats believed in the *Animi Mundi* (world-soul)—similar to C. G. Jung's description of a collective unconscious. He wanted to resituate Christianity within the context of the perennial philosophy, whereby the world is seen a multi-layered tableau of signs, symbols, and semiotic sub-texts. "As above, so below" (a correspondence between Heaven and Earth). The major arcana of the Tarot presents an array of figures and faces from the unconscious, which allow for the play of coincidence. The Tarot offers a template, a blueprint for wholeness. Through the Tarot we connect to another world beyond our own.

Meditations on the Tarot: A Journey into Christian Hermeticism is a 670-page tome written by an "anonymous author" who was born in Russia in 1900, became a disciple of Rudolph Steiner before converting to Catholicism. The

Synchronicity

author has been identified as Valentin Tomberg (1900–1973). His twenty-two meditations take the form of letters to an unknown friend. The book was published posthumously in 1973. The German translation of 1983 contained a preface by theologian Cardinal Hans Urs von Balthasar. The English translation contained an Afterword by this one-time Jesuit. In the *Meditations*, the author avers that the Tarot pack is laden with the symbolism of Christian hermeticism (a religious and philosophical tradition based upon the writings attributed to Hermes Trismegistus) and that, like the *I Ching*, synchronicity (from the Greek: "*syn*" = "together," "*kronos*" = "time," and "ity" = *quality of*) is the key to reading the Tarot cards. It is when mind (psychical) meets matter (physical)—a point between internal awareness and external events. One enquires: How do the dream-like pictures of the Tarot meaningfully connect to my life? Life may be seen as a living Tarot—when you see the universe through the lens of synchronicity. Synchronicity is a meaning-making process (we give meaning to a sequence of events).

- Acausal = no cause and effect. A-causality: something (B) follows something else (A), but A does not cause B (even if they appear so related).
- Meaning = our interpretation; our mind putting a value on something.
- Coincidence = unrelated events, accidentally conjoined (only appear to be arranged/ordered/planned); when two or more events seem related but are not.

Archetypes (partial personalities) organize and structure psychic imagery into patterns/motifs. We meet the presence of these archetypes in the images of each card of the major arcana (meaning "mystery"), such as the Magician, Emperor, High Priestess, etc. Synchronicity suggests parallelism of time and meaning (the concept of correspondence between physical and psychical realities, as we said). In *Recollections*, Viktor Frankl relates one example he experienced of synchronicity. He was passing by Vienna's Votic Catholic Church, which Frankl loved because it was pure Gothic. Elly—his wife—and Dr. Frankl heard organ music and he suggested they go in. As soon as they entered the music stopped and the priest began to preach from his pulpit. He spoke of the nearby Bergasse 19 and of Freud—"the godless Jew" who lived there. Then he said: "But we do not need to go so far, not to Bergasse. Right behind us, at Mariannengasse 1, lives a Viktor Frankl who wrote a book, with the English edition title *The Doctor and the Soul*—a godless book indeed." The priest tore the book to shreds. Later, Frankl introduced

Dynamics of Discernment

himself, a bit worried that this encounter might give the poor priest a heart attack! "How miniscule is the chance that I would enter at exactly the moment when the priest mentioned me in his sermon?"[2]

The Tarot is similar to the *I Ching* in that in both there is an interdependence of objective events and subjective states. Synchronicity is not chance, not causality either, but a deep, subtle, secret wisdom, a constellation, a cross-linking, a correspondence, or continuum whereby macrocosm and microcosm converge, drawing physical and psychical phenomena together. The patterns that emerge appear as "confluences." The Self—not contained by the ego or limited by space or time (the process by which the *psyche* lives out its inner nature) is an inherent part of each synchronistic event.

> "There is no such thing as accident; it is fate misnamed."—
> Bonaparte Napoleon

Symbols resonate in the depths of the human *psyche*. There is an intimate link between symbol and *psyche*. "Seeing-as" (duck or rabbit? below) is the essence of symbolism.

Source: Wittgenstein, *Philosophical Investigations*, **204.**

> "True philosophy entails learning to see the world anew."—
> Maurice Merleau-Ponty

> "My destination is no longer a place, but a new way of seeing."—
> Marcel Proust

> "The whole of life lies in the verb seeing."—Pierre Teilhard de Chardin

2. Frankl, *Recollections*, 59.

"Through our eyes, the universe is perceiving itself. Through our ears, the universe is listening to its harmonies. We are the witnesses through which the universe becomes conscious of its glory, of its magnificence." —Alan Watts

If you imagine twenty-one cards in the shape of a triangle, seven cards on each side, a point in the center of the triangle represented by the zero card, and a square around the triangle (consisting of fifty-six cards, fourteen on each side), you get a representation of the relation between God, man, and the universe. The Triangle is God (the Trinity, or the noumenal world). The point is man's soul. The square is the phenomenal/visible world, which is contained in man's consciousness. The fifty-six cards as a whole represent . . . a complete picture of all the possibilities of man's consciousness.

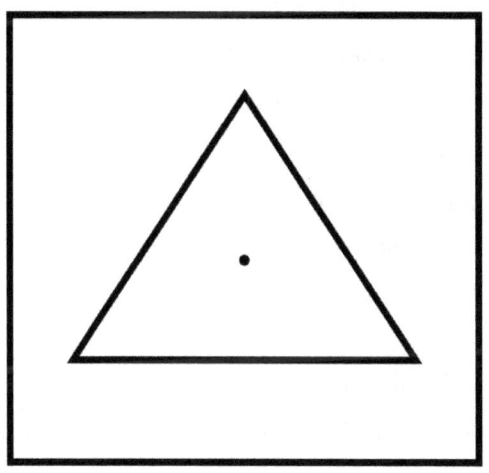

The Twenty-two cards:

Zero The Fool
I The Magician
II The High Priestess
III The Empress
IIII The Emperor
V The Pope/Hierophant
VI The Lover(s)

XI The World
XI Force
XII The Hanged Man
XIII Death
XIIII Temperance
XV The Devil
XVI The Tower

Dynamics of Discernment

VII The Chariot   XVII The Star
VIII Justice   XVIII The Moon
VIIII The Hermit   XVIIII The Sun
X Wheel of Fortune XX Judgement

The Tarot cards can be used for creative brainstorming and decision-making. (No focus on hocus pocus!) Let us repeat, they are *not* about fortune telling or foreseeing the future. Each card contains an evocative symbolic image. The Tarot is a way of generating insights (inspiration through illustration) through free-association and amplification. The layout of cards is known as "spreads." Each card can suggest an approach to creative problem-solving, a plan of action.

- Wands: intentions, goals, agendas
- Swords: decision-making, logic, strategies
- Cups: emotions, feelings, intuitive perceptions
- Coins: practical matters, resources, money

So: decisions (Swords) made to save money (Coins) could impact the morale (Cups) of a company's employees, for example. The following are a set of instructions:

- Select a deck.
- Shuffle and deal the cards.
- Create a spread—lay them out in a straight line, a cross or circle.
- Creatively play.

"Reading the cards" involves meaning-making.

1. Prepare for the "reading" (space and time for creative thinking)
2. Phrase a question
3. Select a spread
4. Shuffle the deck
5. Cut the cards
6. Deal the cards
7. Interpret the cards

Synchronicity

(Suspend the inner critic; think symbolically). Exercise: draw a card, and tell a story about what you see. List all the objects, images, symbols, then jot down an association to each one. The Tarot can be used for business, relationships, critical thought, decision-making, problem-solving, brainstorming possibilities, goal setting, action-planning etc. Let your mind roam free. The spread can be used as a five-card sequence, for example, to help make a decision in life:

1. Your motivation
2. Ideal outcome
3. Your values/principles
4. Option 1: likely outcome
5. Option 2: likely outcome

This is a structured exercise. But you can always just shuffle and spread a few cards out and look at them and see what emerges for you, like a Rorschach test. Decipher it as you would a dream. What is capturing your attention? What are the symbols showing? Think of the cards as twenty-two advisors. You may pick the Fool; enquire: what would the Fool do? Perhaps you need to bring some fun and humor to the situation at hand. Or, what would the Hermit do? The Fool could symbolize playfulness and inexperience; just as the Magician might symbolize creativity and skill. Card 20 is Judgement: decisions. Whether it be a single card draw or a spread, each symbol on the card can speak to you imaginatively, providing you with a gamut of options and creative choices. What do you see? The cards communicate symbolically with your subconscious. They help you envision alternatives so that *you can make your own future*. Let us look at the symbolism of the Trumps:

0. Fool: enthusiasm and inexperience
1. Magician: empowerment and creativity
2. Priestess: reflection and reception
3. Empress: development and growth
4. Emperor: authority and directives
5. Hierophant/The Pope: externals and regulations (tradition and convention)
6. Lovers: affiliations and partnerships

7. Chariot: victories and triumphs
8. Strength: resolve and focus
9. Hermit: solitude and isolation (sabbatical)
10. Wheel of Fortune: cycles and fluctuations
11. Justice: evaluations and deliberations
12. Hanged Man: trials and transformation
13. Death: transitions and endings
14. Temperance: mediation and blending
15. Devil: manipulation and selective vision
16. Tower: destruction and revision
17. Star: hopes and goals
18. Moon: mystery and fears
19. Sun: sensation and satisfaction
20. Judgement: decisions and conclusions
21. The World: completions and realizations

Synchronicity

Synchronicity, as we have been saying, is the simultaneous occurrence of events which appear significantly related but have no discernible causal connection. Jung discussed these ideas with Albert Einstein before World War I, but first introduced the term "synchronicity" publicly in a 1930 lecture in reference to the *I Ching*. His research was subsequently published as *Synchronicity: An Acausal Connecting Principle* (together with a related study by Nobel physicist Wolfgang Pauli, with whom he had a long correspondence). Synchronicity characterizes the simultaneity of events that are not causally connected. The proposition put forward is that there is an interdependence between the physical universe and the *psyche*. This postulate which, if true, has far-reaching consequences, has been attacked as well as applauded.

1. Events may be connected by causality.
2. Events may be connected by meaning.

Synchronicity

Synchronicity operates by way of number two above. Spurious correlations? Or parallels with aspects from relativity theory and quantum mechanics? Is the universe a *cosmos* (deep order—wholeness—*undus mundus*) or chaos (consisting of random chance mutations)? These are the questions.

In *Synchronicity*, Jung gives a number of examples from his own experience of synchronistic events. On Friday, April 1st, 1949: Jung had fish for lunch; someone mentioned "April fish"; that same morning Jung made a note of an inscription which read: "*Est homo totus medius* piscis *ab imo*" ("the whole fish from the bottom center"); in the afternoon, one of Jung's patients, whom he hadn't seen for months, showed him paintings of fish; in the evening, he was shown an embroidery with fish-like sea monsters on it; and the following morning, a patient reported that she had dreamt of a large fish swimming straight at her. At this time, Jung was engaged in the study of the fish symbol in history. The suspicion is that this was a case of meaningful coincidence, even though, for Jung, it seemed to have a numinous quality. It is odd that the fish theme recurs no less than six times within twenty-four hours. According to Jung, events may be linked either through causal chains or meaningful cross-connection. Synchronicity seems to be bound up with the archetypes, which constitute the structure of the collective unconscious, that is to say, a *psyche* identical in all individuals (the Self-same source).

Another example of Jung's is this: he was treating a young woman who had a dream, at a critical juncture in her analysis, of a golden scarab. While she was telling Jung of the dream (he was sitting with his back to the closed window), he heard a noise behind him, like a gentle tapping, and turned around to see a flying insect knocking against the windowpane from outside. Jung opened the window and caught the creature in the air as it flew inside—it was a scarabaeid beetle, the nearest analogy to a golden scarab that one finds in those latitudes. So, for Jung, meaningful coincidences rest upon an archetypal foundation. There are many examples of the simultaneous occurrence of two meaningfully but not causally connected events in his book.[3]

Synchronicity thus consists of *two* factors:

- An unconscious image comes into consciousness directly or literally or indirectly (symbolized or suggested) in the form of a dream, idea, or premonition (ESP).

---

3 In addition to Jung, *Synchronicity*, see also Progoff, *Jung, Synchronicity, and Human Destiny*.

Dynamics of Discernment

- An objective situation coincides with this content.

Such cross-connection of events as Jung and others have described cannot be explained causally, so the hypothesis can be entertained of one and the same transcendental meaning manifesting simultaneously in the human *psyche* and in the arrangement of external and independent events, a view which conflicts of course with conventional science. The synchronicity principle asserts, therefore, that the terms of a meaningful coincidence are connected to *simultaneity* and *meaning*. There is cause and effect—and there is meaning. According to Chinese philosophy, there is the *Tao*—God, or meaning, or the Self, or divine Providence, which Lao-tzu describes thus:

> "There is something formless yet complete
> That existed before heaven and earth.
> How still! How empty!
> Dependent on nothing, unchanging,
> All pervading, unfailing.
> One may think of it as mother of all things under heaven.
> I do not know its name,
> But I call it "Meaning."
> If I had to give it a name, I should call it "The Great.""

Chuang-tzu (a contemporary of Plato's) says of the psychological premises on which the Tao is based: "The state in which the ego and non-ego are no longer opposed." Taoists think in terms of the whole. Platonists agree that in the archetypal World, all things are in all. The Spirit that shapes and penetrates all things is the World Soul (*animi mundi*). Expressed in the language of analytical psychology: the microcosm, which contains the images of all creation, would be the collective unconscious—such is the divine similitude. Man is a microcosm or monad enclosing the whole in himself. It was Plato in ancient times who also took for granted the existence of transcendental images or models (forms—*a priori* meanings) of empirical things whose reflections (imitations) we see in the phenomenal world. If there are parallels between *psyche* and *polis* (Plato), there are also crossovers between *psyche* and *physis* (Jung). Space, time, and causality (the triad of classical physics) would then be supplemented by synchronicity: from tetrad to *quaternio*. Out of the Third (law of three) comes the One as the Fourth (see Plato's *Timaeus*).

Synchronicity

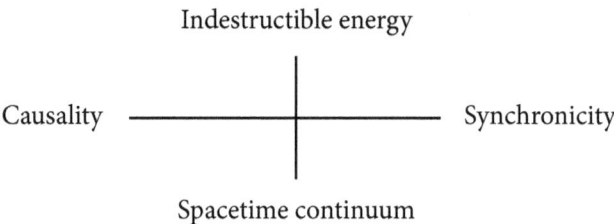

Source: Jung, *Synchronicity*, 98.

If causality is constant connection through effect, synchronicity is inconstant connection through contingence/equivalence/meaning.

"Coincidence is God's way of remaining anonymous."—Albert Einstein

"Noösphere" was Pierre Teilhard de Chardin SJ's term to denote the sphere of spirit and meaning. For Irish Benedictine monk and philosopher, Mark Patrick Hederman, coincidence is one of the ways in which the Spirit makes His presence felt without importuning or interfering with man's free will.[4]

"Life is a journey up a spiral staircase."—W. B. Yeats

The life we lead may be understood as a symbolic journey, a progressive deepening into *psyche*—an act and art of soul-making. Each card and/or toss of the coin depicts the interconnection of inner meanings and outer events, a profound mystical unity, One World, what Frankl labelled "monanthropism" (akin to monotheism). Similarly, physicist Erwin Schrödinger proclaimed, "I am this whole world," while Jung opined, "... the psyche is simply 'world.'" Then we realize that there is no separate self, only one without a second.

"The goal is important only as an idea; the essential thing is the *opus* which leads to the goal: *that* is the goal of a lifetime."—C. G. Jung

---

4. See his book *Walkabout* which details and describes his three-year journey to allow meaningful coincidence to dictate the rhythm and pattern of his life.

6

The Triune Brain

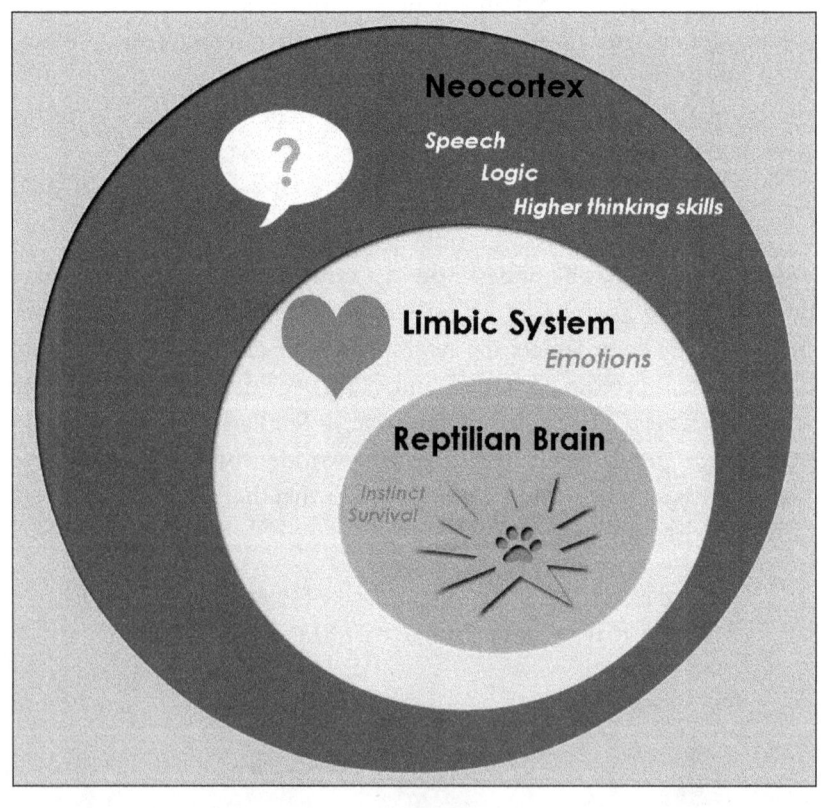

Model of MacLean's Triune Brain Paradigm by Lchunhori at English Wikipedia

The Triune Brain

Source: https://en.wikipedia.org/w/index.php?title=File:Triune_brain.png. Used with no changes under the Creative Commons Attribution-Share Alike 2.5 Generic license (https://creativecommons.org/licenses/by-sa/2.5/legalcode)

THE BRAIN WEIGHS ALMOST three pounds and has 1.1 trillion cells (more than the stars in the Milky Way Galaxy). A neuron makes 5,000 connections with other neurons, establishing a network of 500 trillion synapses. The brain operates 24 hours a day, 7 days a week, 365 days per year. It is fueled by glucose and oxygen. It is a storehouse. Although somewhat out of favor with scientists today, the concept of the triune brain is a sensible (if somewhat simplistic) model. Criticisms can be levelled against the details and minutiae of it, but it has the advantage of clarity and simplicity and is immensely useful for heuristic purposes. Most neuroscientists focus on the two large hemispheres of the brain—the left and right, for example. We may cite in this regard the magisterial work of Iain McGilchrist, *The Master and his Emissary: The Divided Brain and the Making of the Western World.*

Triune theory is a model of the evolution of the vertebrate forebrain and behavior proposed by Paul McLean (1913–2007) who was an American physician and neuroscientist attached to Yale Medical School. He propounded the view that the human brain was in reality *three brains in one*: the reptilian complex, the limbic system, and the neocortex. He originally formulated his theory in the 1960s.

- **Reptilian** (also known as the R-complex or "lizard brain"; basal ganglia; responsible for species-typical instinctual behaviors involved in aggression, dominance, territoriality, and ritual displays).

- **Paleomammalian** (consists of the septum, amygdalae, hypothalamus, hippocampal complex, and cingulate cortex; responsible for the motivation and emotions involved in feeding, reproductive and parental behavior).

- **Neo-mammalian** (consists of the cerebral neocortex cortex, a structure found uniquely in higher mammals and especially humans, conferring the ability for reasoning, language, abstraction, planning, and perception).

To put it in generalized terms:

- Reptilian: instinctual
- Paleomammalian: emotional
- Neo-mammalian: rational

Dynamics of Discernment

The first outer part of our brain is the neocortex which is responsible for rational thinking. The second or middle part is the limbic area which controls emotions and feelings. The third part is the inner amygdala area which is the reptilian brain—the oldest part responsible for, according to some research, 90 percent of our decision-making. It controls our fight-flight response and operates unconsciously. The reptilian brain remembers mostly what happens first and last, in other words, the beginning and end shape the experience, leaving a lasting impression. In terms, let us say of selling something, one should explain not why someone should purchase your product but the opportunity cost of not buying it. The reptilian brain only understands meanings in absolute (black and white) terms. The lizard brain has a survival mentality so any communication should focus on the *benefit* to the client/customer, not the *brand*. To appeal to the reptilian brain, one should convey the message visually—*show* what you are trying to say. (As Wittgenstein noted: what cannot be said, must be shown).[1] Of course, the whole brain is involved in the decision-making process, but the reptilian brain is the driving force. So, in terms of business, it is incumbent to keep the reptilian brain in mind as it will have a long-term effect on the bottom line. Appealing to the reptilian brain can only strengthen any sales strategy. The reptilian brain is the instinctual and the oldest of the three layers of the brain; it has been with us since the very beginning in terms of our evolutionary and ancestral past. It controls the body's vital functions such as heart rate and breathing. It includes the main strands found in a reptile's brain (hence its name): the brainstem and the cerebellum. So, it is associated with our baser instincts such as assessing threats, sexual desires, and survival needs. Unconscious instincts (as Freud and neuroscience have found) can supersede any decision that occurs in the limbic system or neocortex centers of the brain. The limbic system is the emotional part of the brain associated with feelings. It monitors and controls the endocrine and autonomic nervous system. This too plays a part in decision-making. When we are emotionally triggered, we tend not to make the best decisions. The neocortex is the rational part of the brain, responsible for cognition, perception, motor function, spatial awareness, and communication. It has an executive function and plays the role of a CEO when making decisions. But the amygdala can be highjacked and the feeling brain can override the thinking one, causing emotional

---

1. This is a paraphrase of a line Wittgenstein repeated in various ways in his writings. See *Tractatus* for the likely original.

The Triune Brain

flooding. In such cases, our capacity to make wise and effective decisions will be hampered/hindered/highjacked. Indeed, according to economist Daniel Kahneman, the reptilian brain still rules.[2]

Rarely do any of the three layers of the brain operate solely. They often rely on each other. At times, certain layers will override or influence other layers. Scientific studies frequently show that consumers are often more mindless than mindful decision-makers. Many people "go by gut instinct"—this is the reptilian brain at work, when making a decision, rather than engaging with a rational thought process. Because instincts are hard to ignore neuroscience marketing would caution us not to ignore the reptilian part of the brain. When making decisions, it is important to emphasize that we (our rational brains) are not always in complete control. We can make impulsive choices or deliberate too long. As the neocortex decides, it can be overthrown by the reptilian brain intruding/interfering/intervening. Or it confers with our cortexes to influence choices. The emotional brain, for its part, can distort (rational) judgement. The incitement to impulsivity is especially prevalent in teenagers as any parent will attest. This contemporary neuroscientific model of the brain is in accord with ancient philosophy's description of the self. Plato offers a tripartite division of the *psyche* (soul) thus:

- Vegetative soul: plants—reproduction and growth
- Sensitive soul: animals—mobility and sensation
- Rational soul: humans—thoughts and reflection

The difference is the degree of consciousness present in each type of soul. The "soul" is somewhat like the subtle body in Vedanta. From Plato onwards, Western psychologists, have distinguished *three* faculties of the mind—these are philosophical precursors to the triune brain:

- Cognitive (knowing)
- Conative (willing)
- Affective (feeling)

For Plato, there are parallels between soul and society:

- Head: Guardians
- Heart: Warriors
- Hands: Artisans

2. See Kahneman, *Thinking Fast and Slow*.

Dynamics of Discernment

The human soul comprises:

- Appetites
- Emotions
- Reason

Applying these insights to decision-making, one can say that we make *three* types of decisions—instinctual ones that are unconscious, emotional ones, and rational ones. If the midbrain is the hot brain, the neocortex is the cold brain. According to evolutionary psychiatrist and Jungian analyst, Anthony Stevens, the archetypes have their neuronal substrate in the phylogenetically older parts of the brain.[3] Emotion is the energy required for learning: putting that another way, emotion and learning are inextricably interlinked. Now, the combination of *experience* and its accompanying *emotion* creates an *imprint*, a term first employed by Konrad Lorenz (or "archetype" to employ Jung's term from 1919). For Freud, the unconscious is biographical, for Jung it is biological; if for Freud, the unconscious is ontogenetic (our personal past), for Jung it is phylogenetic (the past of the human race).

- Freudian: personal unconscious: acquired (individual)
  —contains complexes
- Jungian: collective unconscious: inborn (universal)
  —contains archetypes

Archetypes are archaic, primordial determinants—universal images, typical dispositions, nodal points within the structure of the *psyche* itself (endogenous) that have evolved through natural selection. The existence of archetypes, according to Stevens and other Jungians, has been amply corroborated by diverse disciplines including mythology, ethology, sociobiology, and evolutionary psychiatry. They can be seen as innate releasing mechanisms (IRMs), to draw on Dutch biologist Niko Tinbergen's description.[4] Now, other analysts, such as existential analyst Medard Boss writes of "existentials" (exogenous) in the Heideggerian sense rather than archetypes in the Jungian sense, but this discussion will have to be parked as it will take us too far afield.[5] For now, let us say, that, for Jung, if the ego is the complex of consciousness, the Self is the archetype of archetypes

---

3. See Stevens, *Archetype: A Natural History of the Self.*
4. See Stevens, *Archetype: A Natural History of the Self*, 39 and 56.
5. See Boss, *Existential Foundations.*

The Triune Brain

or *Ātman* in the language of Advaita, pure, undifferentiated, self-shining consciousness—timeless, spaceless, unthinkable, and indistinguishable from *Brahman* (the Ground of being).

> "Ultimately every individual life is the same as the eternal life of the species."—C. G. Jung

French anthropologist and marketing consultant Clotaire Rapaille, author of *The Culture Code* (formerly a practicing child psychiatrist and psychoanalyst), who draws heavily on the model of the triune brain, adds a "cultural unconscious" to the Freudian biographical and Jungian biological (ancestral) ones.[6] Each culture has its own mindset.[7] According to Rapaille, there are *three* structures we have to take into account:

- Personal script: your unique individual identity (with its infinite variety)
- Cultural archetype: what is acquired (language, art, habitat, history, etc.)
- Biological scheme: we all come from a woman, for example (our DNA)

The "Culture Code" is the unconscious meaning we apply to any given thing, such as a car or food, etc. Rapaille (and his team) organize a structured three-hour session to try to a) understand the product by asking questions of participants about its use etc., b) to hear through creating a collage of words stories about the product, c) to accessing through relaxation and music the earliest memory of the product (the first imprint). The process moves from the cortex (which Rapaille ignores and bypasses) to connect with the reptilian. Imprints alter the reference system of the culture and each culture is composed of countless archetypes. There are *five* principles he works with in uncovering/discovering the culture code:

---

6. The American physician and Jungian analyst Joseph Henderson (1903–2007), who co-founded the C. G. Jung Institute of San Francisco, presented a paper in Zurich in 1962 at the Second Congress of Analytical Psychology entitled "The Archetype of Culture," where, as far as I can adduce, the concept of a "cultural unconscious" was first enunciated.

7. In private communication with the author in response to a question I put in relation to triune brain theory, Rapaille cited the Polish American scientist and philosopher Alfred Korzybski's that "a map is not the territory" and opined that "the scientific understanding of the brain is still in infancy." See Korzybski, *Science and Sanity*.

Dynamics of Discernment

- You cannot believe what people say (because most people don't know why they do the things they do, due to the subconscious at work).
- Emotion is the energy required to learn anything (emotion is the key to learning and imprinting).
- The structure, not the content, is the message (see the work of cultural anthropologist Claude Lévi-Strauss).
- There is a window in time for imprinting and the meaning of the imprint varies from one culture to another (most of us imprint the meanings of significant things by the age of seven).
- To access the meaning of an imprint within a particular culture, you must learn the code for that imprint (the code is a combination that unlocks the door. Every word/action/symbol has a code).

Participants' responses are analyzed/examined after the sessions to adduce the common messages and the code is cracked. So, just to give a few examples from Rapaille's book on countries and coffee first: the French culture code is "I think" (following Descartes) whereas the American one is "I can" (following their philosophy of pragmatism). With coffee, it was found that the important thing was its smell (aroma) not its taste and subsequently advertising campaigns were arranged around this motif. Other ones include the following: the American culture code for seduction is MANIPULATION; for love is FALSE EXPECTATION, for sex is VIOLENCE, for health and wellness is MOVEMENT.[8]

Other marketeers have proposed similar tripartite sequences, such as:

- IQ: Rational   Knowing cognitively; conceptual competence
- AQ: Affective   Knowing how to move people (understanding what people are feeling)
- CQ: Cultural   Knowing what works in different cultures (understanding the local and the global)

There are *four* types of knowing:

- Propositional (example: knowing that energy and mass are equivalent)
- Perspectival (example: knowing what it is like to see the earth from the moon)

8. Rapaille, *The Culture Code*, 7–9.

The Triune Brain

- Procedural (example: knowing how to compose a symphony)
- Participatory (example: knowing how to co-ordinate a team)

But what Rapaille's and other ones that utilize triune brain or archetypal theory (analytical psychology) will have in common is the emphasis on the reptilian brain. The cortex (cerebral hemispheres) comes into play at approximately the age of seven, handles learning and abstract thought, while the limbic system, which is structured between birth and five years of age, deals with the emotions, as we said, and these two can wage war within, producing, in the words of existential psychoanalyst, R. D. Laing, a "divided self."[9] The "undisputed champion," as Rapaille puts it, of the "three brains" is the reptilian brain.[10] In a battle between logic and instinct, the reptilian brain wins out, he contends. Why this is important and relevant to our foregoing discussion is that we do not usually have any awareness of our subconscious behavior and the "real" reasons behind the choices and decisions we and/or others make.

Undecidability

This is a postmodern "PS" by way of conclusion. "Undecidability" is not apathy; it is not being paralyzed like a deer caught in a headlight. Rather than an inability to act, undecidability is the condition, according to contemporary Continental philosopher Jacques Derrida, of acting and deciding. When a decision is really a decision—and more than a programmable, deducible, calculable, result of a logarithm—it has passed through the ordeal of undecidability. The "opposite" of undecidability, therefore, is not "decisiveness" but calculability. For Derrida, decision-making depends upon undecidability, which gives us something to decide. When deciding, one looks into the abyss and makes a leap of faith. One gives oneself up to the impossible decision.

> "Only a decision is just."—Jacques Derrida

What is just is the singular situation and the instant of the decision. So, the ghost of undecidability hangs like a specter over all decision-making, according to Derrida. It is never set aside or done with. It hovers over a situation before, during, and after the decision, disturbing it from within, divesting it

---

9. Laing, *The Divided Self*.
10. Rapaille, *The Culture Code*, 74.

Dynamics of Discernment

of arrogant self-assurance. However difficult the decision or undecidable the situation, justice is always demanded now. Such is a just decision's urgency. It does not wait. However, much time is expended in deliberation, a just decision requires an expenditure without reserve. We choose/decide in the dark, in fear and trembling, *sans* criteria. We act in the night of dark knowledge.

> "The instant of decision is a madness."—Sören Kierkegaard

The Single One (individual) is always driven to insanity by the System ("the crowd is untruth. Truth is subjectivity"). In the final analysis, no-one else can make a decision for you, least of all "the They".

A decision is an alignment. I decide to do what I do, to be there where I am, to no longer let things be imposed upon me (abdication/hijacking). *Decisions are discoveries*. Revelations. Transformations. They bid me to be otherwise. The effect is liberation. The "will" is active in wanting, wishing for such and such. It involves a choice and a consequence. A decision is more of a consequence (frequently unknown) than a choice. We do not know what we are getting ourselves into. All sailors know that one commands the wind only by obeying it. We can always change the way we decide. It does not always have to be from one's personal preferences. When deciding, we undergo an experience that can change us. We forge ahead or we forgo. We commit without knowing what the future we are choosing will be like. As authentic agents we match our choice with our preferences, to the kind of life that realizes our hopes and aspirations, but frequently something else sounds through us, something less individual and more universal or transpersonal.

I wish you well, dear reader, with all your choices, discerning, and decision-making. We must decide for weal or for woe what to make of our life—whether we live it out encased in ego which would be a tragedy or ethically engaged in self-transcendence. One way or the other, whether we flourish or flounder, our existence contains the seeds of monumental meaning.

> "In the concentration camps, . . . in this living laboratory and on this testing ground, we watched and witnessed some of our comrades behave like swine while others behaved like saints. Man has both potentials within himself; which one is actualized depends on decisions but not on conditions."—Viktor Frankl.

Let the last word go to American poet Shel Silverstein, who in *The Voice*, aptly sums up the still, small, gentle nudge/prod of the Self that orients us to truth, freedom, and fullness of life:

> "There is a voice inside of you
> That whispers all day long,
> 'I feel that this is right for me,
> I know that *this* is wrong.'"

Bibliography

Almaas, A. H. *Keys to the Enneagram*. Boulder, CO: Shambhala, 2021.
Anonymous. *Meditations on the Tarot: A Journey into Christian Hermeticism*. Afterword by Hans Urs von Balthasar. New York: Penguin, 1985.
Boss, Medard. *Existential Foundations of Medicine and Psychiatry*. New York: Jason Aaronson, 1977.
Chestnut, Beatrice. *The Complete Enneagram*. N.d.: She Writes, 2013.
Costello, Stephen J. *Between Speech and Silence*. Eugene, OR: Pickwick, 2022.
———. *The Nine Faces of Fear*. Eugene, OR: Pickwick, 2022.
Easwaran, Eknath. *Essence of the Upanishads: A Key to Indian Spirituality*. Toronto: Nilgiri (The Blue Mountain Center of Meditation), 2009.
Eger, Edith Eva. *The Choice: Escaping the Past and Embracing the Possible*. New York: Scribner, 2017.
Frankl, Viktor. *The Doctor and the Soul*. London: Souvenir, 2004.
———. *Man's Search for Meaning*. 5th ed. London: Rider, 2004.
———. *On the Theory and Therapy of Mental Disorders : An Introduction to Logotherapy and Existential Analysis*. Translated by James M. DuBois. New York: Brunner-Routledge, 2004.
———. *Recollections: An Autobiography*. Translated by Jospeh Fabry. Cambridge, MA: Basic, 2000.
———. *The Will to Meaning: Foundations and Applications of Logotherapy*. New York: Meridian, 1988.
———. *Yes to Life: In Spite of Everything*. Boston: Beacon, 2020.
Freud, Sigmund. "Creative Writers and Day-Dreaming." In *The Freud Reader*, edited by Peter Gay, 436–42. New York: Norton, 1995.
———. *The Ego and the Id*. Edited by Terri Ann Geus. Dover Thrift Editions. Mineola, NY: Dover, 2018. Originally translated by Joan Riviere and published by Hogarth and the Institute of Psycho-analysis, 1927.
Grogan, Brian, SJ. *Making Good Decisions: A Beginner's Guide*. Dublin, Veritas: 2015.
Guo, Kristina L. "DECIDE: A Decision-Making Model for More Effective Decision Making by Health Care Managers." *The Health Care Manager* 27 (2008) 118–27.

Bibliography

Harvard Business Essentials. *Decision Making: 5 Steps to Better Results*. Boston: Harvard Business School, 2006.

Heath, Chip, and Dan Heath. *Decisive: How to Make Better Decisions*. New York: Random, 2014.

Hederman, Mark Patrick. *Tarot: Talisman or Taboo?: Reading the World as Symbol*. Dublin: Currach, 2003.

———. *Walkabout: Life as Holy Spirit*. Dublin: Columba, 2005.

Holmes, Edward. *The Life of Mozart: Including His Correspondence*. New York: Harper & brothers, 1845.

Hopkins, Gerard Manley. *As Kingfishers Catch Fire*. New York: Penguin, 2015.

Horan, Daniel P. *The Franciscan Heart of Thomas Merton: A New Look at the Spiritual Inspiration of His Life, Thought, and Writing*. Notre Dame, IN: Ave Maria, 2014.

Hudson, Russ, and Don Riso. *The Wisdom of the Enneagram*. New York: Bantam, 1999.

Hume, David. *A Treatise of Human Nature*. Vol. 1. Edited by David Fate Norton and Mary J. Norton. Oxford: Oxford University Press, 2007.

Irvine, William. *Aha!: The Moments of Insight that Shape Our World*. Oxford: Oxford University Press, 2015.

Iyengar, Sheena. *The Art of Choosing*. New York-Boston: Twelve, 2010.

Judkins, Rodd. *The Art of Creative Thinking*. London: Sceptre, 2015.

Jung, C. G. *The Archetypes and the Collective Unconscious. The Collected Works of C. G. Jung*. Vol. 9. Edited by Herbert Read. Translated by R. F. C. Hull. London: Routledge, 1991.

———. *C. G. Jung Letters. Vol. 1: 1906-1950*. Edited by Gerhard Adler and Aniela Jaffé. Translated by R. F. C. Hull. Princeton, NJ: Princeton University Press, 1973.

———. "Commentary on *The Secret of the Golden Flower*." In *Psychology and the East* 3-58. Princeton: Princeton University Press, 1978.

———. *Memories, Dreams, Reflections: An Autobiography*. Edited by Aniela Jaffé. Translated by Richard Winston and Clara Winston. London: Fontana, 1995.

———. *Synchronicity: An Acausal Connecting Principle. The Collected Works of C. G. Jung*. Vol. 8. Translated by R. F. C. Hull. Bollingen. Princeton: Princeton University Press, 2010.

Kahneman, Daniel. *Thinking Fast and Slow*. New York: Farrar, Strauss and Giroux, 2013.

Kaufman, James C., and Ronald A. Beghetto. "Beyond Big and Little: The Four C Model of Creativity." *Review of General Psychology* 13:1 (2009) 1–12.

Kavanagh, Patrick. *The Complete Poems*. Newbridge, Ireland: Goldsmith, 1972.

Korzybski, Alfred. *Science and Sanity: An Introduction to Non-Aristotelian Systems and General Semantics*. Fifth edition. Forest Hills, NY: Institute of General Semantics, 1995.

Krogerus, Mikael, and Tschäppeler, Roman. *The Decision Book: Fifty Models for Strategic Thinking*. London: Profile, 2017.

Laing, R. D. *The Divided Self: An Existential Study in Sanity and Madness*. New York: Penguin, 1965.

Leibnitz, Gottfried Wilhelm. *New Essays Concerning on Understanding*. Second edition. Cambridge Texts in the History of Philosophy. Edited by Peter Remnant and Jonathan Bennett. Cambridge: Cambridge University Press, 1996.

Lévinas, Emmanuel. *Totality and Infinity: An Essay on Exteriority*. Translated by Alphonso Lingis. Pittsburgh: Duquesne University Press, 1969.

Lewis, C. S. *The Problem of Pain*. New York: Harper One, 2001.

Bibliography

———. *Surprised by Joy: The Shape of My Early Life*. New York: Harper One, 2017.
Lonergan, Bernard. *Insight: A Study of Human Understanding*. Edited by Frederick E. Crowe and Robert M. Doran. Toronto: University of Toronto Press, 1997.
———. *Method in Theology*. Toronto: Univeristy of Toronto Press, 1971.
Maitri, Sandra. *The Spiritual Dimension of the Enneagram*. New York: Penguin Putnam, 2001.
Mann, Leon, et al. "Effectiveness of the GOFER Course in Decision Making for High School Students." *Journal of Behavioral Decision Making* 1 (1988) 159–68.
May, Rollo. *The Courage to Create*. New York: Norton, 1975.
———. *Man's Search for Himself*. New York: W. W Norton, 1953.
McElroy, Mark. *Putting the Tarot to Work: Creative Problem Solving, Effective Decision Making, and Personal Career Planning*. Minnesota: Llewellyn, 2004.
McGilchrist, Iain. *The Master and his Emissary: The Divided Brain and the Making of the Western World*. New Haven, CT: Yale University Press, 2009.
McLean, Paul. *The Triune Brain in Evolution*. New York: Springer, 1990.
Michalko, Michael. *Thinkertoys*. Berkeley: The Speed, 2006.
Moser, Drew. *The Enneagram of Discernment*. Beaver Falls, PA: Falls City, 2020.
Murdoch, Iris. "On 'God' and 'Good.'" In *Existentialists and Mystics: Writing on Philosophy and Literature,* edited by Peter Conradi, 337–62. New York: Penguin, 1997.
———. *The Sovereignty of God*. London: Taylor & Francis, 2013.
Nichols, Sallie. *Jung and Tarot: An Archetypal Journey*. Maine: Samuel Weiser, 1980.
O'Brien, Paul. *Visionary I Ching Cards: The Book of Changes for Intuitive Decision Making*. Hillsboro, OR: Beyond Words, 2020.
Ouspensky, P. D. *The Symbolism of the Tarot*. Los Angeles: IndoEuropean, 2010.
Paul, L. A. *Transformative Experience*. Oxford: Oxford University Press, 2014.
Pigliucci, Massimo. *How to Be a Stoic*. New York: Basic, 2017.
Progoff, Ira. *At A Journal Workshop*. New York: Penguin Putnam, 1975.
———. *The Dynamics of Hope*. New York: Dialogue, 1985.
———. *Jung, Synchronicity, and Human Destiny: Noncausal Dimensions of Human Experience*. New York: Delta, 1973.
———. *The Symbolic and the Real*. New York: Julian, 1963.
Rapaille, Clotaire. *The Culture Code*. New York: Crown Business, 2007.
Rilke, Rainer Maria. *Letters to a Young Poet*. Translated by M. D. Herter Norton. New York: Norton, 1973.
Saint-Cyr, Viviana M. "Sublimation in Lacan: The Creative Destruction of the Subject." *Psychoanalytische Perspectieven* 28 (2010) n.d.
Salecl, Renata. *Choice*. London: Profile, 2010.
Sartre, Jean-Paul. *Existentialism and Humanism*. Translated by Philip Mairet. London: Methuen, 1948.
Scharmer, Ott C. *The Essentials of Theory U: Core Principles and Applications*. CA: Berrett-Koehler, 2018.
Scheler, Max. "Ordo Amoris." In *Selected Philosophical Essays,* translated by David R. Lachterman, 98–135. Northwestern University Studies in Phenomenology and Existential Philosophy. Evanston, IL: Northwestern University Press, 1973.
Schwartz, Barry. *The Paradox of Choice: Why More is Less*. New York: Harper Perennial, 2004.
Solzhenitsyn, Aleksandr. *The First Circle*. London: Harvill, 1988.

Bibliography

Spardough, J. Michael, SJ, et al. *What's Your Decisions: How to Make Choices with Confidence and Clarity: An Ignatian Approach to Decision Making*. Chicago: Loyola, 2010.
Stevens, Anthony. *Archetype: A Natural History of the Self*. London: Routledge, 1982.
Tetlow Joseph A., SJ. *Always Discerning: An Ignatian Spirituality for the New Millennium*. Chicago: Loyola, 2016.
Thibodeaux, Mark E., SJ. *God's Voice Within: The Ignatian Way to Discover God's Will*. Chicago: Loyola, 2010.
Wagner, Jerome. *Nine Lenses on the World*. Evanston, IL: NineLens, 2010.
Wallas, Graham. *The Art of Thought*. Kent, UK: Solis, 2014. First published in 1926.
Weil, Simone. *Simone Weil: An Anthology*. Edited by Sian Miles. New York: Grove, 1986.
Wilhelm, Richard. *The I Ching or Book of Changes*. Translated by Cary Baynes. Princeton: Princeton University Press, 1957.
Winnicott, Donald. *Playing and Reality*. London: Routledge, 1971.
Wittgenstein, Ludwig. *Philosophical Investigations*. Translated by G. E. M. Anscombe. Oxford: Wiley-Blackwell, 2009.
———. *Tractatus Logico-Philosophicus*. Translated by D. F. Pears. New York: Humanities Press, 1974.
Wolff, Pierre. *Discernment: The Art of Choosing Well*. Missouri: Liguori, 2003.

www.ingramcontent.com/pod-product-compliance
Lightning Source LLC
Chambersburg PA
CBHW072154160426
43197CB00012B/2384